TESTIMONIALS FOR EVEROLD REID and
THE REID METHOD

"Last October Everold changed the way I looked at Lexus, and his commitment to service and accountability is the reason I don't hesitate to recommend him to colleagues looking to buy a luxury vehicle. At the time, we were looking to replace my wife's Venza. I had owned five Acuras over twelve years and had no intention of switching. However, Everold's customer-first approach and commitment to "make things right" truly proved he was interested in my needs as an ongoing customer and not just in the initial sale. He's unquestionably the best sales rep ever."

— *Howard Morton, CEO & Managing Partner,*
Boardwalk International Advisors

"We purchased a Sienna from Everold this week and it was the best purchasing experience ever! Everold was consultative, listened to our needs, was knowledgeable about all aspects of the trade-in and purchase process and made us feel great about our decision. Thank you for a great buying experience!"

— *Dave Miller, Worldwide Enterprise Sales-Dynamics*

"Dear Everold,
I would like to take this opportunity to thank you very much for all your efforts to accommodate my most recent situation with my car lease.

I have purchased many cars in the past and dealt with a number of very professional salespeople.

You have, however, exhibited greater levels of professionalism, problem solving, creative selling and resourceful financing solutions. You have also displayed a strong client orientation without disregarding the interests of Lexus. In short, you are an outstanding salesperson! Congratulations!"

— *Carlos Avilés*

"Everold was very interested in understanding my needs and went above and beyond to demonstrate how important my business was to Lexus. I felt like a valued customer even before making the purchase. Because of that I trusted his recommendation and believed that he was providing me the best deal possible. When you connect with and can trust your consultant, you're more inclined to make the purchase. I would personally like to recognize Everold and to thank him for a great and seamless experience."

— *L. Ritchie*

"I have known Everold for over twenty-four years while he worked at another dealership. In 2008, Everold came to work for me as my sales manager at Oakville Toyota and that year we had a record sales year. As the business continued to grow, I acquired another franchise, Lexus of Oakville. Everold was given the task to open Lexus of Oakville as general sales manager and in our first year we exceeded every target given to us by Lexus Canada and won the prestigious award of excellence.

Everold eventually became my 'go to' person as there was no task he could not complete successfully and, while doing so, he trained his colleagues at the same time.

I cannot recall ever meeting anyone who has been more focused and goal-oriented than Everold. He is able to accomplish and exceed any goal he has been given, while able to work under pressure and stay calm and focused."

— *Frank Apa, President, Lexus of Oakville*

THE
REID
METHOD

To Alan -
Continued Success

TRM.

THE
REID
METHOD

A BLUEPRINT FOR SALES MASTERY

EVEROLD REID

MILNER &
ASSOCIATES INC
· EDITING · PUBLISHING · COMMUNICATIONS · CONSULTING

Library and Archives Canada Cataloguing in Publication Data
Information is available upon request

Production Credits
Preliminary edit: Ross Fattori, Rosswords Advertising, Consulting
        and Publishing
Editor: Karen Milner
Interior design and typesetting: Adrian So
Cover design: Amy McIntyre
Printer: Friesens
        IngramSpark (POD)

Published by Milner & Associates Inc.
www.milnerassociates.ca

Printed in Canada
10 9 8 7 6 5 4 3 2 1

CONTENTS

FOREWORD

By Mike "Pinball" Clemons

In greatest part due to phenomenal teammates and quality coaches who demanded the most of me, I am a Hall of Fame football player who became a history-making coach. Beyond that, and most importantly, I am a husband and a dad. One of my primary passions today is philanthropy and, with the generosity of our numerous supporters, the Michael "Pinball" Clemons Foundation (MPCF) provides schools, scholarships and housing in Canada and in developing countries around the world.

It is this passion for philanthropy that first connected me and Everold Reid, the author of this book. Everold initiated and drafted a marketing relationship between MPCF and Lexus of Oakville, his employer and a generous supporter of MPCF and the schools we build. That marketing relationship marries passion, purpose, profile, branding and image to create a partnership that continues to thrive today.

My support of this book is embedded in the author's proven performance for more than two decades. Navigating challenging economic and cultural shifts in different regions and countries, he's continued to innovate and outperform industry standards. In fact, in the fields of auto sales, advertising and marketing, Everold is a true champion. That's a bold statement for a sports guy, but all we have to do is check his statistics to confirm that he's an all-star.

Everold started in auto sales at nineteen years old, and by the time he was twenty-two he had already been elevated to the role of sales manager at a major dealership. In sports terms he was the Rookie of the Year. At twenty-seven, he opened his own used-car dealership, including parts and service departments. Successful but a real grind, and he was easily recruited back to his first love, sales. He then propelled a stagnant dealership to a record sales performance, garnering national attention. You could say this was his first championship. He went on to more big wins: He was chosen by Lexus of Oakville to open a new dealership, which won the prestigious President's Award; he surpassed every corporate target he was given; he championed a multi-million dollar international marketing firm; and he led every dealership and marketing team he was part of to a breakthrough performance.

And, even in his current role as a consultant, he continues to exercise his sales muscles—although he's too modest to admit it, he not only helps Lexus of Oakville to implement effective marketing strategies and mentors his peers, he also still leads the team in sales every year . . . amazing!

Some twenty years ago, in a conference of big ideas, I heard a wonderfully articulate and accomplished female IBM executive assert, "Imagination without execution is chaos." I certainly don't want to undermine the need for new ideas that stimulate creativity; they are the catalyst of innovation. In fact, this book has many great new ideas. But in a world where time is at a premium, we need more than ideas—we need a plan. And, as the title suggests, this book is not just a plan but a methodology, a proven approach, a blueprint for success.

Undoubtedly, you see why I emphatically urge the serious salesperson, and anyone who wants to learn how to execute effectively, to acquire this book. Everold Reid is an all-star, a repeat champion in the world of auto sales and in the advertising and marketing industry. Learning from him how to improve your sales technique and your marketing strategies is akin to Sidney Crosby teaching you to score goals, Tom Brady mentoring you to play quarterback or Serena Williams teaching you to play tennis. They are not just people who know how to get it done, but icons who are still at the top of their game.

Everold Reid has proven over many years that he is not only a top performer himself, but that he can also coach others to improve their results and themselves. I still don't know why he would not keep these ideas, plans and processes to himself and his dealership. Instead, he has chosen to share his knowledge and the secrets of his success in *The Reid Method: A Blueprint for Sales Mastery*. Now everyone who reads this book and follows its approach can benefit from Everold's mentorship.

In retrospect, that is probably why I chose to work with him from the start: because he is a great salesman, and an even better man.

ACKNOWLEDGMENTS

I won't bore you with a long list of thank yous and have the background music drive me off the stage as if I'm accepting an Academy Award. I will, however, thank three very important people who have helped to shape my life personally and professionally.

First, to my Aunt Brenda, a teacher who, along with my late, great-grandmother, took care of me while I lived in Jamaica from my early toddler days through around age ten, while my mom, Denese, sought a better life for me in Canada. They provided me a solid foundation from which I gained knowledge, understanding and learned the fundamentals of family and taking care of each other, as well as kindness to others in need.

Secondly, to my Aunt Paulette, another teacher whom I lived with when I returned to Jamaica to live there through my high-school years, before returning to Canada to live with my mom for the second time. Here, I was able to grow into a young man, learning responsibility and the need to have an education, goals and ambition.

Both my Aunt Brenda and Aunt Paulette would exemplify manners and respect for others, which I try to instill in my own kids today. I remember these early years vividly, and often reflected on them while I was writing this book.

Finally, to Paul Pearson (a former owner of Erin Park Lexus Toyota), the man responsible for giving me a big career opportunity when I was only twenty-one years old. That opportunity in sales management at a young age is largely responsible for my career path and success today. Paul saw something in me at the time that I didn't know I had: a gift to communicate and win clients and peers over, to negotiate, and a relentless approach to get the job done and get results.

To these three individuals I owe a great deal, and I am happy that I can share this book with them all today.

INTRODUCTION

As the saying goes, you never know where life will take you. I can tell you that at no time in my life have I ever aspired to writing a book, but here I am writing a book on sales strategy and psychology in the wee hours of the morning, before going off to a new day of sales and leasing opportunities at a new car dealership near Toronto, Canada.

My career in the retail auto industry began in August 1989, when I took a summer job selling cars while attending Centennial College in Scarborough, Ontario. I was enrolled in the aircraft maintenance program and my chosen path at the time was a far cry from car sales. I aspired to be an airline pilot.

I love airplanes—always have. Even today, the theory of flight and airplanes are all-consuming passions. I've documented over 100 hours of flight time as a learning private pilot and have flown as a business traveler on commercial flights over 700 times to date.

But as a nineteen-year-old young man living on his own, that summer job in automotive sales quickly became a full-time necessity to survive.

Other responsibilities came with the job as I quickly rose through the ranks, from sales representative to assistant sales manager and then to sales manager within two years. Before turning twenty-three, I had earned two managerial promotions; and I led our sales team to record-setting sales performances before I was twenty-five years old. I was voted one of the top Toyota sales managers in our dealer group, and a top sales manager among dealers across Canada; I also won the president's choice first prize, including an award of $5,000 for 1995 sales, which was a lot of money then.

At first I started working with a domestic dealership, and shortly thereafter I joined a major Japanese brand, Toyota. The differences in the products and philosophies were obvious. I quickly learned about Kaizen, the Japanese philosophy of continuous improvement, which Toyota consistently applied to all of their team members, products and services.

I embraced the Kaizen philosophy and began making continuous improvements in my own daily practices, in the core principles of my work and in learning about sales, especially as it related to the automotive industry. I remember using the old PAL (Personal Activity Log) books long before the Internet or specialized software and adapted them through trial and error. They were an early attempt to improve sales success, largely through looking at the numbers rather than considering other, broader skill sets.

The PAL system included twelve monthly log books for individual sales representatives, and a sales manager edition for tracking the entire sales team. One of the best features of the PAL book system is that it measures a sales representative's performance against their own personal goals or benchmarks, creating a personalized coaching resource for sales reps and managers to use in working together towards increased sales. The PAL book system is still offered and used today in many dealerships, but more seasoned sales professionals create, as I do, their own tracking system using Excel spreadsheets with varying levels of matrixes. (We'll discuss different methods of benchmarking and tracking in more detail in several chapters later in the book.)

The Kaizen philosophy has also influenced my involvement in philanthropy. Years ago, I realized the importance of giving back to the community and I've worked continuously since then with local groups to share the fruits of my good fortune.

For example, at the dealership where I work, I initiated a partnership with the Michael "Pinball" Clemons Foundation (MPCF), a non-profit organization dedicated to promoting health and education in communities locally and around the world. Some of the proceeds from each car delivered to our clients go directly to MPCF to support the good work that they do.

I also formed a partnership between our dealership and Kerr Street Mission (formerly Kerr Street Ministries), a local Oakville-based cooperative that provides services for people living in economic, social and spiritual poverty.

As of mid-July 2015, the dealership and I have entered the third year of our philanthropic relationship with Kerr Street Mission and MPCF, with almost $50,000 CDN in donations made to date, directly from sales and deliveries of vehicles to our customers. We continue to find more ways to further our involvement in the local community with the Kaizen philosophy in mind—always trying to improve on what we are doing, even in philanthropy.

The automotive business has changed tremendously since 1989, and I've been on the front lines to observe those changes. The retail car industry has evolved from a cut-throat, price-driven business with no social media or online presence, to a hyper-competitive industry with a plethora of vehicle models and choices, and with all-time low interest rates and creative incentive programs.

In fact, in some respects it's more difficult to sell or lease a vehicle now than it was twenty years ago. Today, thanks to the vast amount of information available to consumers, car shoppers are highly educated about our products and services—and about the numerous closely competitive models on the market—making the selling process more challenging for dealerships and their sales staff. It's quite normal now for customers to be more informed about makes, models, specifications and ratings than the salespeople they're talking to.

Clients today narrow their search down to a few models and gather all the facts about those choices well in advance of calling the dealership or visiting a showroom. Before all this widespread access to information, clients made up to four or five visits to showrooms to gather information before purchasing. Today's potential clients may make only one to three visits because they have such easy access to so much information themselves, on their computers at work and at home, or on mobile devices.

I stepped away from the auto industry for a while, turning to the world of advertising and marketing for eight years between 2004 and December of 2011. When I returned to the automotive retail industry in January 2012, I was shocked how little had changed in terms of the internal sales processes, and the skill level and professionalism of the sales staff. It was as if everything—including the cars, dealer facilities and the use of technology—was better, but the sales techniques had not evolved to keep up with the changing customer needs and buying habits.

But, regardless of changes in technology or competition, I learned there are some fundamental reasons why clients make a decision to buy a particular product or service, and from whom. I needed to understand why, and I needed to know how to convert potential customers to clients. In short, I needed to understand and answer the why and the how questions of sales.

> There are some fundamental reasons why clients make a decision to buy a particular product or service, and from whom.

Now I can see why, back in 1989, I thought that if I could figure out the key components of why potential clients decided to buy our product or service, and if I could understand the psychology of buying, I could make this a career and just not a job.

And so, with every client, over many years, I made mental notes and recorded my ideas and observations in various places, which ultimately leads me to writing today, *The Reid Method: A Blueprint for Sales Mastery*. I thought if I could share the successes I've had using the sales methods in this book, I could offer my twenty-five years of experience and insights to benefit other individuals, dealerships and sales groups, helping them to be better prepared for their own successes. This book will be beneficial to sales professionals at every level:

- Provides new sales reps a fundamental path to success.
- Offers tools and strategies to help the average salesperson move to the top of their game.
- Shows top salespeople how to maximize their full potential by working smarter and not harder.
- Gives sales managers practical advice they can use in training and coaching their sales reps to improve their skills and achieve their goals.

My hope is that the proven methods outlined in this book will help any salesperson or sales manager to grow in their role and achieve success in their career.

CHAPTER 1

CHOOSING AUTOMOTIVE SALES AS A CAREER

While many view a career in auto sales as a job filled with long, tiring hours and the need to employ strong closing techniques with everyone who walks through the dealership doors, a career in auto sales can actually be fun and very rewarding. You can earn a good, six-figure income with many other benefits, while meeting and dealing with many interesting people every day.

If you're outgoing, charismatic and like meeting new people, then you may be a good candidate for a career in automotive sales. You must jump into this role with both feet, giving it your all and keeping an open mind to learn as much as possible and not just focusing on the money first. This approach will work in any sales environment, selling any product or service. After all, selling is about providing a product or service and addressing the client's needs to the best of your ability by providing them with advice, options, a fair price and after-sales follow-through.

A BRIEF HISTORY OF AUTO SALES:
A LOOK BACK TO THE 1990S

The business of automotive sales is nothing like it was twenty years ago. The days of showing up to a dealership wanting to sell cars with fast-talking, hard-closing techniques to make a quick buck are over. Succeeding in this industry nowadays requires certain basic fundamentals, such as character, an obvious inner drive and the desire to serve other people's best interest before yours.

The old sales model—which included cold calling, qualifying leads, many more test drives, hard closing techniques and marathon negotiations—has been replaced by a new sales model of engaging a more educated clientele and creating a positive purchase and service experience. To master this new sales model, you need greater product and market education, including a basic knowledge of social media.

Consumers are equipped with far more knowledge than ever before and come armed with mountains of research already done online by the time they walk into a dealership, so you need to be at least as engaged and knowledgeable as they are. Beyond that, professionalism, courtesy, friendliness, integrity and, most importantly, accountability are all minimum requirements today. So if you approach a career in auto sales as nothing more than a good way to practice closing skills, you will find little success and much frustration.

In the 1980s and 1990s, automotive sales were predominantly driven by numbers. It was about moving cars over the curb and earning big commissions, especially when selling used vehicles, with little emphasis on creating a positive purchase experience and excellent customer service. With fewer regulations and oversight then, the automotive business was sometimes ruthless in its practices, and some even bordered on illegal. It was those practices that led to stereotyping of the aggressive, overbearing used-car salesperson. Today the automotive industry is heavily regulated, with an emphasis on ethics, fair competition and transparency, especially in marketing, advertising and representation to consumers.

In reality, during the 1980s and 1990s if you had a pulse, decent attire and could steer or convince clients with your limited communication skills—and you did not have a criminal record—you could be hired to sell cars. You could wing your way through the process with client after client until you got better through trial and error, or made too many mistakes and got fired.

From the dealers' point of view, it was more about getting the most gross profit on a new or used deal by adding options, accessories and after-sales products, such as rust proofing or warranties. Often this approach meant negotiating for hours to make a deal, just so the client could get an extra hundred dollars off the price of the car, or an extra five dollars off per month on a lease or finance payment.

In the 1980s and 1990s, a better deal was more often than not defined by who left whom more worn down over sometimes aggressive and lengthy negotiations primarily focused on price and payment terms. It was about who could outlast the other in the negotiations. I remember having clients who set aside hours to negotiate over just a few dollars every time they bought from me, and I would dread wasting half my shift on just one client.

In the 1980s and 1990s, a better deal was more often than not defined by who left whom more worn down over sometimes aggressive and lengthy negotiations.

Making deals in the eighties and nineties was more numbers-focused with less emphasis on what *value* the potential client was actually getting, and certainly less concern about customer service or CSI scores (Customer Service Index). In fact, I don't remember dealing with customer surveys much at all until the turn of the millennium, when more focus was placed on customer service. That's when competition began to heat up and new entrants like Hyundai and Kia were becoming more popular in the North American marketplace.

In fact, customer service was an afterthought for a long time and this contributed to a negative stereotype for the automotive industry, which still lingers today.

SALES PROFESSIONALS NEED TO BE . . . PROFESSIONAL

Stiffer competition across the board these days means that there is a greater need than ever for good sales professionals in the automotive industry. More competition and more similarities among makes and models of cars means that the primary way for a dealership to differentiate itself and to be successful is to offer a higher caliber of customer service and a better customer experience.

But good sales professionals are hard to find, whether they are aspiring or experienced salespeople. While pricing may no longer be the major point of negotiation, consumers are more inclined to buy from someone they like and trust rather than someone they don't make a genuine connection to. That all-important first impression, connection and rapport are vital to a successful career in automotive sales.

If you're considering a career in automotive sales, or have recently entered the business, it's very important to know the ground rules and fundamentals or you will spin your wheels and have limited or no success.

For those who would like to give it a shot and are just starting out, auto sales in general offers very good earning potential and benefits. A base salary plus commissions is typically offered;

in addition, most salespeople receive company-subsidized health and dental family benefits and, after a probationary period, either a car allowance or a company demonstrator vehicle. The total salary ranges will depend largely on location, branding, dealership business model or philosophy, marketing strategy and, of course, the most important factor: you, the aspiring sales professional—your experience, attitude, skills, and your willingness to continuously develop and improve in your role.

Even with the right expertise and abilities, your success is not guaranteed. Most of all, it's important to have the right mind-set to have a chance of succeeding and not just surviving. To excel in a sales role, it's essential to maintain your own core principles, to remain open to learning, and to adapt best practices that you encounter along the way, either through formal training or simply observing others who are good at what they do.

Survivors usually take shortcuts, whereas successful salespeople take every example as a learning experience to grow and improve.

Survivors usually take shortcuts, whereas successful salespeople take every example as a learning experience to grow and improve. They will have goals and objectives and many other tools, such as training audio CDs, DVDs or books, to keep their minds stimulated and to gain an edge by picking up new ideas all the time. The goal of a sales representative who wants to be successful is daily progress, which brings confidence.

Those who do well in sales usually have the potential of moving on or moving up. For example, many sales professionals who earn success at one dealership are recruited away to similar roles with other higher-end brands or higher-volume dealerships. Other sales stars are given the opportunity to move up into sales management; but not all sales professionals are interested in management, and not all good sales professionals make good managers either. Career advancement and landing a new job with a new employer should mean an increase in compensation, and may yield better perks, including a nicer company car, prizes like trips and better working hours or conditions.

THE INFORMATION REVOLUTION AND THE AUTO SALES INDUSTRY

The Internet, and more precisely the rapid advancement of consumer access to the Internet, represents a tremendous change in auto sales and in sales within other industries. What was once a mystery, such as the cost pricing of automobiles, is now readily available to anyone with Internet access and some very basic computer search skills.

For example, there are many new companies whose core business model is providing clients with access to cost and dealer margins in exchange for a small membership or subscription fee online. This kind of information service provides your potential client the convenience of obtaining final prices, or guiding them to their vehicle of choice, long before they arrive at the showroom. Many dealers today have dedicated departments that handle only leads from such subscriber services and from the Internet in general, so they can handle the significant increase in online shoppers.

Dealerships and other sales organizations that adapt and manage this additional aspect of their business can be highly successful and very efficient. This is a fast-growing profit center in most dealerships and retail businesses, often becoming the most efficient department in today's retail business environment, thanks to the lower overhead required. In most cases, all that's needed is a small Internet sales staff, handling the larger volume of inquires just by emails and phone calls.

Widespread consumer access to pricing and other information may seem like the beginning of the end of automotive sales careers, with dealerships needing only to post their pricing on the vehicle windows and have someone on staff to answer product questions, handle test drives and help customers fill out paperwork. However, this is far from reality.

While potential clients today will usually research extensively online and make phone calls to verify information and narrow down their selection, once they start making calls or visits to a dealer showroom, they're now looking for the right person to guide them through completing the process they already started.

Now it's even more important than ever to be prepared, as potential clients are armed with much more information.

What has changed is that this part of the buying process is much shorter than before. So now it's even more important than ever to be prepared, as the potential clients are armed with much more information. Your potential client will already have narrowed their choice of vehicles by researching areas such as safety ratings, fuel consumption ratings, cargo and passenger capacity, FWD or AWD options, etc. What normally would have required multiple dealer visits and test drives now may require only two or three visits, and the salesperson who usually gets the deal is the one who makes a genuine connection with the client, by taking interest in the client's needs and best addressing them—and all while maintaining a great attitude.

GROW YOUR BUSINESS BY GROWING YOUR PERSONAL SKILLS

In the chapters ahead you will learn core principles, discover best practices and understand a clear pathway for how to turn a sales

job into a successful career—and have fun doing it. You will learn
about the fundamentals of sales that, if practiced consistently,
will lead you to ultimate success in automotive sales, or in any
sales career.

Some of those key fundamentals, such as being obsessed
with delivering excellence and loving what you do, will help you
understand your role fully, and can make all the difference in
your day-to-day success—in having clients drawn to you or being
referred to you constantly.

You'll learn core principles, discover best practices and
understand a clear pathway on how to turn a sales job into a
successful career.

You will understand why having the right attitude is not at all
about being phony and pretentious, but rather about being genuine so that clients appreciate and connect with you. You will
learn how to build raving-fan clients who will stick with you for
many models and years, and will refer many additional buyers to
you, helping you to grow your personal client base.

In any sales career, it's a huge asset to grow your client base
and that should be your focus from day one. Finding ways to
grow your personal client base every chance you get takes care
of the future times when factors beyond your control (such as a
slowing economy) affect sales.

You want to have an established base so that more clients
are calling you, instead of you constantly chasing new clients.
Your existing clients will themselves upgrade to newer vehicles
or products, and they will also refer multiple new clients to you,
ensuring that you can continue to expand your customer base.
You certainly want referrals because they come already primed
and ready; referrals are usually much easier closes because someone else recommended you and already helped to establish trust.

You'll learn why dressing for success along with a positive attitude are a winning combination of looking the part and fitting the role as a professional while making that all-important first impression. And you'll learn how establishing trust after getting past the first-impression stages will be one critical rule that you must practice as part of establishing and building that long-term client base. Building trust with your customers will ultimately assist you in cultivating that repeat and referral business that's so crucial to growing and succeeding in any sales career.

At the end of the day, it's about being prepared. Preparation starts with you being obsessed with delivering excellence and loving what you do. Preparation is having the right attitude and dressing the part to make your best first impression. Preparation is planning every day so you can best address the client's needs first. Preparation is getting ready for an appointment by studying competitive models, having a test-drive vehicle ready and being available when your clients show up.

In the past, test driving a vehicle and having that vehicle wow the client would often sell the car; or showing off any other kind of new, fancy product would be enough to make the sale. However, in today's competitive marketplace you may test drive the car or demonstrate the product well, but you may not end up being the one who closes the sale because you lacked preparation and there is no genuine connection between you and the potential client. You did not make a good enough first impression and you're not clicking with that client or they're not clicking with you.

You cannot and won't sell to everyone, even if you do all the preparation in the world, but chances are significantly higher that clients will do business with you and remember you if you're well prepared, professional and easy to do business with. There's a lot of poor service out there, and differentiating yourself as genuinely trustworthy, professional and knowledgeable is a great way to ensure your customers will have a much more positive experience, and a much more lasting relationship, than they would elsewhere.

So, the formula to increase your chances of success is to deliver a consistent positive attitude and professionalism. Your clients will appreciate the interest you take in them and the knowledge and advice you offer to affect their decision.

The other big factor in today's sales environment that I've learned the hard way is that you better not be distracted. Pay close attention to the client you're with and give them the attention they deserve. Don't take calls or check text messages when you're talking to a client. It's rude and disrespectful. Today's tech-savvy consumers are social-media driven, detail-oriented, and have many other choices and outlets if you don't treat them well and give them your undivided attention. If they're not happy with the level of attention and engagement from you, you can be sure that they'll spread the word to their entire network.

Almost all the vehicles I sold and advertising deals I made across North America were as a result of making a connection with a client.

Some connections were made immediately, once a client visited the showroom and something sparked a conversation about sports or something unrelated to cars; but there was always some mutual interest that broke the ice. This works even better when you make calls to potential clients in their offices or homes, where you walk in and can immediately pinpoint a conversation piece, whether that's an award, sports memorabilia, pictures, accomplishments, etc.

In the following chapters, you will get a clear understanding of a proven formula for ultimate success in sales and precise examples that will boost your sales career.

Take it from someone who's been in the automotive sales business since August 1989. I've been selling successfully for twenty-five years. As a matter of fact, for the 2013 calendar year I sold over 200 new and pre-owned vehicles and delivered 191 of them through retail, all non-fleet deals consisting mostly of leases. And that wasn't my only responsibility. I did this while actively overseeing marketing and advertising initiatives for two car dealerships, mentoring and training other staff and spearheading community and charitable events. Being organized helped me to manage all these other responsibilities while still selling and leasing over 200 vehicles.

When you lead by example your colleagues will naturally gravitate to you for advice and strategy, guidance and certainly encouragement.

In 2013, I could have sold and delivered at least fifty more vehicles had selling been my primary focus. But for our main dealership I was solely and directly involved with delivering at least twenty-eight percent of the dealership's total sales while mentoring two other sales representatives through the year as well. It was well noted that my direct sales, along with those made by the two other colleagues whom I mentored, contributed to over fifty percent of the dealership's sales in 2013.

In 2014, I delivered a total of 167 vehicles, down a bit from the year before as the Toyota dealership was sold in March 2014 and we endured construction of a new Lexus facility until June 7, 2014. And at the halfway mark in 2015 I had already sold and delivered 90 units on a six-month goal of 100, again while still involved with many other duties as mentioned before.

It's very gratifying to me that not only am I able to keep delivering top sales results, but that I am also able to help others improve their results as well. In fact, I never actively sought out my role as a mentor, but when you lead by example your colleagues will naturally gravitate to you for advice and strategy, guidance and certainly encouragement. They wanted to know why I led the sales board most months and how they could improve their sales results as well.

SEVEN STEPS TO SALES SUCCESS

If you choose sales as a career, you will need to do the following to achieve success:

1. **First, choose a product or service you love and appreciate.** It's very hard to sell anything that you don't really believe in because that emotion can slip through and may often cost you deals. If it's car sales, choose a brand with a proven track record and that you like. If you truly believe in a product or service, then more genuine emotion will flow from you to your potential client and that positive energy will actually help you sell. Plus, it's simply more enjoyable for you to present a product that you can back up with confidence, and your enthusiasm will resonate with the prospective client.

2. **The second thing you must understand and practice is preparation—for yourself and your workday.** In today's marketplace, it's critical that you make a positive first impression, starting with your dress code and grooming. This is even before you greet a prospect. Starting off on the right foot comes down to a very basic, but essential, disciplined approach because your potential client will size you up in a matter of seconds. Research shows that within ten seconds of you greeting someone new in a professional role, they have already formed an opinion of you. You really do have only one opportunity to make that great first impression, so it's crucial that you put your best foot forward.

   For example, you should never greet a client when you smell like a smokestack or you've doused yourself with too much perfume or cologne. With today's smoke-free environments, people find it offensive to indulge a smoker who reeks of second-hand smoke, even if that smell is masked by perfumes or colognes.

Grooming and preparing yourself physically is the first significant part of getting ready for your day and boosting your self-confidence out of the gate. After that, you must also prepare mentally for your workday. Preparing your workday should include organizing and prioritizing tasks, appointments and checklists. In the next chapter, I will provide key principles for preparing and organizing your workday for ultimate success.

3. **Thirdly, you must have goals.** Goal setting forms the basis from which to plan for and accomplish ultimate success. Those goals must be realistic, implementable and measurable if you are to have a hope of realizing them. For example, you can express your goals in terms of the income, volume or sales goals you eventually want to achieve, and then break them down into monthly and daily targets or assignments.

Every workday you must have an action plan to guide you through the day toward your goals.

Every workday you must have an action plan to guide you through the day toward your goals. How many calls and emails will you make and send? Who will you contact today or follow-up with tomorrow? What will be your strategy when you call and email these clients? And what's your message or method to get the appointment and eventually the sale? The message or method must include the fundamental reason for the email or call or you're wasting your time and your potential client's time and it may anger them. This may lead to not being able to contact them again, especially with today's strict anti-spam legislation— and, therefore, to not meeting your larger goals.

Everything you do every single workday is an opportunity to build incrementally towards your goals; it's essential to have objectives to hit, and a plan to get you there each and every day.

4. **Fourth, you must invest in yourself.** This doesn't mean getting into debt and buying the most expensive suits or tools. To invest in yourself means taking time to learn about your field of work and what steps you can take to be better prepared. Again, invest in proper attire and look as professional as you can afford. Next, seek out motivational tools such as CDs and books, and watch motivational speeches on YouTube that are relevant to your situation. Read current publications that are related to your field. Feeding your mind with good information will make you more knowledgeable and will provide you with greater confidence when you meet customers. Remember, clients are reading and researching before they come in to see you. Be prepared.

Some of this material is free and readily available, but I know salespeople who have never picked up a motivational book or tried to educate themselves, and they wonder why they're average at their jobs. Whether you make your sales opportunity a career or a job is directly linked to your ambition and how much you invest in yourself, to learn more about what it takes to continuously improve and stay ahead of the game.

5. **Fifth is being obsessed with your career.** Probably the most consistent positive attribute I've observed in the

most successful salespeople I've met in the past twenty-five years is that they love what they do. In fact they're obsessed with their careers. They love meeting new people every day and they love the thrill of making deals. Liking your job may provide you with a modest living, but being excited about it and fully engaged can make all the difference between mediocrity and ultimate success.

Success is contagious and clients like dealing with people who are successful. More than a few times, I've had clients buy just because of the exercise and thrill of making a deal, although they did not need or want the car or advertising I was selling. They bought because I came across as enjoying what I was doing and they felt engaged in the process of making a deal. A successful salesperson is confident, prepared, motivated, organized and possesses a great attitude. You can tell just by looking at them.

6. **Sixth, and probably the most important of all, is attitude.** I bet you've heard that before. Your attitude will dictate your ultimate level of success. With any job, big or small, with any client, with any relationship, with any co-worker, with any superior, having the right attitude makes all the difference in the world. A salesperson with a positive attitude is open to (and adapts to) change, and accepts constructive criticism in order to improve in their role. Clients appreciate a positive attitude; in fact, it helps right away to establish trust.

7. **The seventh step is practicing daily personal discipline and staying focused and motivated.** Discipline can make the difference each day, each week and each month between great successes and average or poor results. This

starts from when you wake up each morning to go to work. Your everyday rituals can put you in the state of mind necessary for a good working day. For example, your workday should always start by eating right. A healthy diet keeps the mind focused throughout the day, as you deal with each client and the challenges you'll face.

Remember, for the most part you're using your brain in your work, and you can get very tired using your brain all day. You need to have a sharp mind, enhanced focus and concentration, especially when listening to clients' needs, crunching numbers and negotiating. Everything from eating well to being mindful and focusing on actively listening to your clients will help you to stay alert, attentive and energized, no matter how crazy your workday gets.

Now that we've discussed the major, general principles for sales success, in the next chapter we'll focus on the seventh step above: the discipline it takes to become better in your sales role. I truly believe that great sales professionals are made, not born, so let's learn what it takes to train yourself for success every day.

SUMMARY

- **Be committed:** You must jump into your sales role with both feet, giving it your all and keeping an open mind. Learn as much as possible and don't focus only on the money. Aim to make it a sales career and not just a job.

- **Educate yourself:** The old sales model—which included cold calling, qualifying leads, and many more test drives— has been replaced by a new sales model of engaging clients and relationship building—and that requires you to have better product knowledge and market education.

- **The trust factor:** While pricing may no longer be the major point of negotiation, consumers will more likely buy from someone they like and trust rather than from someone with whom they don't make a genuine connection.

- **Work on building and increasing confidence daily:** The goal of any sales representative who wants to be successful is daily progress, to be better than they were the day before—and achieving that builds confidence.

- **Be prepared:** Now it's more important than ever to be prepared because potential clients are coming in much more informed than they have ever been. Your potential client will more than likely already have narrowed down their choice of vehicles by researching the features, performance and value that are important to them. Be ready.

- **Show genuine interest in addressing customer needs:** The salesperson who usually wins the deal is the one who makes a genuine connection with the client by taking an interest in the client's needs and addressing them with a great attitude.

- **Aim to establish trust quickly by building raving-fan clients:** Your loyal customers will stick with you for many models and years, and they will refer many additional buyers to you to grow your personal client base.

- **Make a great first impression:** Learn to fit the role and dress and present yourself as a professional to start every client meeting off on the right foot.

- **Consistently deliver a positive attitude and professionalism:** To increase your chances of success in sales, the simple formula is to show interest in your potential clients and to demonstrate the knowledge and expertise you offer to affect their decision.

- **Do not be distracted:** Pay all your attention to the client
  you're with and give them all the attention required. Do
  not take phone calls or text messages or even check your
  phone. Make them feel that they're the most important
  client at the moment.

- **First choose a product or service you love and appreciate:** If you choose sales as a career, then to have ultimate
  success you will need to first choose a product or service
  you love and appreciate. It's very hard to sell anything that
  you don't really believe in because that emotion will show
  through and cost you deals.

- **You must set goals:** Goal setting forms the basis on which
  to plan for accomplishing ultimate success. Your goals
  must be realistic, implementable and be measurable to
  have a chance of being realized.

- **Have an action plan:** This is what will guide you through
  each and every day towards your goals. How many calls
  and emails will you make and send? Who will you contact
  today or tomorrow? What will be your strategy when you
  call and email these clients?

- **Invest in you:** This doesn't mean getting into debt and
  buying the most expensive suits or tools. Investing in yourself means taking time to learn about your field of work
  and what steps you can take to be better prepared and to
  continuously improve.

- **Be obsessed with your career:** Probably the most consistent positive attribute in the successful salespeople I've
  met in the past twenty-five years is that they love what
  they do.

- **Maintain a positive attitude:** I bet you've heard this before. Without a positive attitude, don't even bother fooling yourself; your attitude will dictate your ultimate level of success.

- **Stay focused and motivated:** Discipline can make the difference each day, each week and each month between great successes and average or poor results. Self-discipline starts when you wake up each morning to go to work.

CHAPTER 2

EIGHT PRINCIPLES FOR A SUCCESSFUL (SALES) CAREER

A disciplined approach to the business of sales is always best and you should not leave home without it. Many people are attracted to sales because of the thrill of the hunt and the appeal of deal making. It's exciting, you have to think on the fly to respond to customers' needs, questions and objections; and, in fact, you have to be a bit of a maverick to be good at it. But the people who truly excel at sales are those who apply structure and discipline to the role, those who set themselves up to learn, improve and succeed.

While sales may be psychological, goal-driven and competitive, the discipline that it takes to be successful must be consistent and must be at your core. True high-achievers will always suggest that lasting success doesn't generally come from making a few big deals or having a couple of big accounts, but more so from the discipline of doing the little things consistently, even though they may sometimes be a bit boring.

If you practice a disciplined approach to sales, with a renewed sense of urgency every shift and every day, implementing best practices will become easier. Discipline in your work life is an essential prerequisite for success in today's sales environment, and starts with certain key routines and basic practices, such as starting the day off right with a nutritious breakfast, laser-like focus, and a plan of action, as mentioned in the previous chapter.

When practiced as part of your daily work routine, rituals put you into a prepared state. Without rituals, you're always out of sync and playing catch-up. At most dealerships and auto retailers, being in sales sometimes requires very long hours, especially during promotional events, and it's easy to get overwhelmed by your day, flustered and off track. Incorporating the discipline of practicing daily rituals is crucial to managing your time, and your own success.

We'll get into much more detail on the principles to follow later in the book, but for now here's an overview of the eight most important disciplines for you to practice frequently and consistently.

1. GET AN EARLY START

Make sure you start your shift or workday off at least fifteen to twenty minutes ahead of schedule. This is a great discipline for anyone to observe, not just salespeople. It allows you to arrive at work cool and collected instead of frazzled and rushed, and it doesn't hurt to be perceived as punctual, dedicated and enthusiastic by those you report to.

The early bird gets the worm is an even greater truism in sales. Being early for your shift in an automobile dealership environment is not only smart for all the reasons above, but is also a great opportunity to meet service clients who are usually hanging around in the showroom. They are occasionally pacing the showroom while waiting for their vehicle to be serviced and could be your next customer.

Preparation for your shift before it actually begins is also crucial to your day flowing well, and in giving you the confidence to handle whatever may come at you. Start your workday by having a routine or practicing a daily ritual. No matter how small, good, consistent habits lead to the bigger results and ultimately contribute to success. It's the little things that eventually make a big difference and those boring details do matter.

Making room in your schedule every day to manage your time efficiently leads to you being more productive and making more money.

Your daily pre-shift routine should at a minimum include setting up your voice mail with a daily greeting and times of availability. Keeping the out-of-office messages on your email updated should also be standard practice, as those alerts tell your clients you've thought about these details and are courteous and organized. This helps them to plan according to your schedule instead of just showing up when you're not there or busy with another client. These two practices should be done the minute you get into the office, or remotely from your smartphone. There's no excuse not to be organized. Making room in your schedule every day to manage your time efficiently leads to you being more productive and making more money.

2. BE ORGANIZED

Clients like to deal with other organized people and tend to choose salespeople who are busy and professional.

In my sales career, I rarely had clients I'd already been in touch with (by phone, email or in person) just show up. Of course there are always clients who will walk in unannounced, but I've always tried to communicate to prospects that the best way for me to provide the appropriate level of service is to schedule an appointment.

Making appointments is a key organizational discipline to practice, and your clients truly appreciate that level of professionalism in today's busy world. You'll quickly find that appointment-based clients yield a higher closing ratio because they're more prepared for the appointment, and you should be as well—ready to meet your client at the appointed time with all your research done ahead of time.

The best way to provide the appropriate level of service is to schedule an appointment.

At some dealerships and retailers, the hours can be very long and the shifts plentiful, so seek employment at a dealership known for heavy traffic so you can use your time effectively and be kept busy with lots of appointments. Or commit yourself to using any downtime you do have in your day to improve the effectiveness of your "up time" by implementing better organizational rituals.

Get in the habit of using any downtime to invest in being better by following up with prospects, researching the competition, increasing your product knowledge, making CSI calls, keeping a tidy work environment, and developing creative personal marketing strategies.

3. LISTEN UP

Once you're past the greeting stage and are engaged with your client in the showroom and at your desk, then it's time to practice the third and most important discipline of sales: listening.

This is where you begin to win the client's trust by listening carefully to their needs and concerns so that you can respond appropriately to their specific individual situation.

Listening is crucial, as the clues to the sale are usually found in the feedback you get from clients. You will learn the reasons for their choices, their priorities and the important features they require. Give your full attention when you're listening, and probe for more information with relevant and adequate questions. Also affirm what they're saying so you can clarify or confirm the situation, their needs and the desired outcome. All clients are different and each deal is structured differently, so each customer's needs and concerns must be given the individual attention they deserve.

4. ADVISE, DON'T SELL

The fourth key principle is all about how you respond to the customer's questions or concerns. It is much more effective to convey information instead of trying to convince or shove your answer or point of view down your client's throat. Clients want to feel that you've got their back and will act with their best interest in mind.

I receive many detailed client comments and compliments weekly about my not being pushy, and thanking me for listening, understanding and guiding them to a positive outcome and decision. This may mean not closing the sale with every client, but leaving a good impression may bring referrals and future business—even from clients who don't initially buy from you.

5. ADD MORE VALUE THAN ANYONE ELSE CAN OFFER

The fifth best practice, and an increasingly important one, is creating added value for your customers. We live in a service-oriented culture today, where clients are shopping for a salesperson. They're looking for someone who can adjust quickly to their needs and personality and can connect with them. All clients are different and you have to adjust to their style accordingly. So the bottom line here is, add more value than anyone else can offer!

Adding more value doesn't mean giving away the farm. Value can be simple and low cost to you, but valuable to your client. Remember, value is perceived, so always have a value proposition for each client, appropriate to their needs and priorities.

Some ways to add value can be as simple as giving a brief tour of your facility to outline the conveniences available to customers, such as express lube lanes, free car washes, night drop-offs, shuttle service, extended service hours and courtesy cars. Other value ideas can include showing your clients special equipment used during the service process, such as high-tech alignment and tire machines.

Show off as many value-added features as possible; pointing them out explicitly could give you an edge over the competition, as many dealers and retailers lack or fail to express value-added perks. Just remember what's important to each individual customer you're dealing with and don't spend time highlighting features and conveniences that are of no interest to them. There's no point going on about your latest high-tech service equipment when your customer is far more concerned about the conveniences available in your waiting lounge, or that a shuttle or loaner car is available when service is required.

We live in a service-oriented culture today, where clients are shopping for a salesperson.

By far the best value you can offer is what you offer of yourself, by showing your clients that you've been listening, and then presenting options and scenarios that are best for them. The value to the client is the fact they will leave with their expectations exceeded, not just met. You will become their "go to" contact for anything related to auto sales because they've built a bit of trust with you. This is how you achieve and build raving-fan clients: by offering not only your company's products and services, but more of yourself than anyone else.

6. DISCOVER THE CLIENT'S REAL WANTS AND NEEDS

To address client needs and to convey information effectively, you must develop the skill of processing and analyzing needs based on what you hear (as discussed in discipline number three above). You usually know when clients are warming up to trusting you when they start relaxing in your office and the conversation digresses to mutual interests like family, sports and sometimes even personal stories.

Beyond listening actively and attentively to understand what your customer is telling you, the sixth principle goes even deeper than that to uncover their real needs, some of which may even be unspoken. Discovering a client's real, underlying needs and wants means being disciplined and committed to guiding them in the right way and making them feel comfortable with the sales experience at the same time.

This ability comes from experience but is also a natural trait of aspiring sales professionals. It starts with practicing and developing ways to clue in on what your potential client really wants—one client at a time—and probing to understand what they really are trying to accomplish as the end result.

We're all clients ourselves and are all purchasers of other products and services, so you gain this experience as a consumer yourself every day. It's a small world, so leave every guest or client with the best impression every time. You never know whom they might refer to you, or whom they know that you're already in touch with. Start with how you like to be treated as a consumer, and think of excellent experiences you've had with salespeople who somehow got to the root of what you were truly looking for, even if you didn't completely realize it yourself. Drawing on your own experiences as a consumer and integrating the best sales practices of others can help you to improve your own technique and the sales experience your clients have with you.

How are you greeted at your local gas station or coffee shop? Does someone make a small difference in your life each day and put a smile on your face just by passing by for five minutes? Why do you keep going back to the same dry cleaners for example?

We all have favorite restaurants and stores that we frequent, and the main reason for frequenting these places comes down to being comfortable with how you're helped and served and the products and services provided. If you weren't satisfied, you would shop elsewhere. Automobile sales and service are no different. Fine-tune your approach with these fundamental principles in mind and make a better effort to understand the client's needs.

Take for example a loyal client of our Lexus dealership. Seventy-nine years old and retired, he had just leased his fifth consecutive Lexus vehicle, the top flagship model to be specific. But just three months after the most recent lease, he was back looking to switch to yet another vehicle. Why did he want to make a change so quickly? Was he not satisfied with the luxury vehicle he had recently leased and which had seemed to fill all his needs and wants? With a little gentle probing, I discovered that the real reason he had to explore downsizing was due to a major financial restructuring. It could be embarrassing for some clients to admit to having financial difficulty at that age, so I took the time to listen to him and to assess the situation carefully and diligently. Due to the client's comfort level in dealing with me and our dealership, I was able to gather the facts to then make my best recommendations. It's always best to uncover the full scope of the issues to know where your opportunity lies. Probing the situation gently and respectfully can help you to uncover the real issues beneath the surface.

7. BE A TEAM PLAYER

The seventh principle involves your teammates or coworkers but still has a direct effect on your overall success. How you deal with clients can also reflect whether you are a good ambassador for your company or product, and how good a teammate you are. Your clients will usually notice the pride you take in your company, product and teammates, and they can sense if everyone is working together, helping and supporting each other, all focused on the common goal of creating a better experience for the client.

Too many salespeople, rookies in particular, are more preoccupied with cashing a commission check than with providing the highest level of service for the client. A good sales professional focuses on the bigger picture, the client's best interest and satisfaction. Taking care of the client's interest first, while being a good company and product ambassador and a good teammate, will guarantee a much more successful long-term career. Clients notice a customer-focused attitude, and they reward it with more referrals and repeat business, which can ultimately lead to promotions or bonuses for the salesperson who thinks about others first.

8. EVERYONE IS A LEADER, EVEN YOU

Lastly, the eighth principle is leadership. Leadership doesn't only mean running the company or being the sales manager; leadership also means directing your own conduct with discipline, taking responsibility and being accountable, and setting a good example for others through your actions.

It's easy to say that each and every one of us can and should
be a leader to some degree, but leadership is often hard to demonstrate as not everyone naturally possesses leadership qualities.
However, good sales professionals can become good leaders by
learning from the example of others. It naturally takes some
leadership skills to be successful and incorporating some of the
best practices of leaders you admire, and maybe even report to or
work with, can help you improve and develop in this critical area.

Discipline is an important part of conducting yourself as a
leader, and the eight principles discussed in this chapter will take
you well down the road to becoming a good leader. Leadership
is many things and can be as simple as being fifteen to twenty
minutes early for work to get prepared and organized. Leadership
is raising the level of expectations and taking action to meet or
exceed them. Leadership is assisting others in your company by
sharing some of your successful methods and strategies to promote individual and overall company growth.

I practice sharing every day. In my current leasing role, I've
created a marketing strategy through an internal contact management system, whereby we contact existing lease and finance
clients up to twenty-six months before the maturity of their lease
or finance contracts. (The previous system contacted clients only
at six months and one year from maturity, which in today's active
marketplace is often too late.) This long lead time is designed to engage our existing clients early enough, and provide them with new
alternatives and additional lease terms, getting to them well before
our competition ever could. We provide an opportunity to clients
to upgrade their vehicles to newer models for similar or sometimes
even lower payments, and clients appreciate these options.

This is a program that I've now implemented throughout the
dealership so that other sales and leasing staff can benefit by
turning over and building their individual portfolios, while maintaining a bit more control of their client base as well.

The end result of sharing this best practice openly is that the dealership enjoys a significant increase in lease renewals; and the sales staff deliver more vehicles, make more money and continue to build their individual portfolio.

You can also demonstrate leadership through philanthropy—getting involved in the community and charitable causes. This could be simply doing volunteer work, or championing a cause and raising money or donations for it, perhaps even influencing your company to become a sponsor of community and fundraising events. Personal success and personal leadership often involve taking the initiative as a private citizen to do something for the public good. Former president Bill Clinton champions doing some sort of public good in private life as a duty that more people should practice, as he has done through the Clinton Global Initiative (CGI), assisting hundreds of millions worldwide since becoming a private citizen.

Personal success and personal leadership often involve taking the initiative as a private citizen to do something for the public good.

We've now covered eight key disciplines and principles fundamental to being successful in sales. In the next chapter, we'll look at the best practices that separate the top performers from the rest.

SUMMARY

- **Start by having a routine or practicing daily rituals.** No matter how small, good habits consistently observed will lead to bigger results and will ultimately contribute to your success. When practiced as part of your daily work routine, rituals put you into a prepared state.

- **Be organized.** Clients like to deal with other organized people and tend to choose salespeople who are busy and professional, who use their time effectively. Make appointments to structure your day, and use downtime to invest in improving your skills, knowledge and strategies.

- **Third, and the most critical discipline of all, listening.** This is where you begin to win the client's trust by listening to their needs and concerns, and thinking about how best to respond to their specific, individual situation.

- **The fourth key principle is knowing when and how to respond.** It may be more appropriate to advise than to sell; to offer choices and information rather than just hard selling and number crunching to convince a client to make a deal. Clients want to know that you're listening, understanding and guiding them to a positive outcome and decision.

- **The fifth principle, and an increasingly important one, is added value.** The bottom line here is that you must add more value than anyone else can offer in order to build raving-fan clients. Remember, value is perceived and is different from person to person, so always have a value proposition appropriate for each client.

- **Understanding the client's real needs, and being disciplined and committed to guiding clients the right way, is the sixth key principle.** This starts, one client at a time, by practicing and developing ways to clue in on what your potential clients really want, and probing to understand their underlying priorities and objectives.

- **The seventh discipline is being a good teammate, and a good ambassador for your company or product.** How you deal with clients can also reflect whether you are a good company or product ambassador, and a good teammate. Your clients will usually notice the pride you take in your company and product, and whether you and your teammates are working together for the overall good.

- **The eighth and final principle is leadership.** Good sales professionals can become good leaders by learning from the example of others. Being a leader doesn't necessarily mean running the company or being a sales manager, but it naturally takes some leadership skills to be successful, no matter what your role.

CHAPTER 3

BEST PRACTICES OF TOP SALES PERFORMERS

In this chapter you'll discover key reasons why top performers always seem to be busy running their own mini sales businesses within the dealership or sales organization. Top performers are self-motivated, they're trendsetters and natural leaders. They don't wait to be told what to do or to be asked to set goals. They lead by example and they're easily spotted, by peers, their managers and by potential clients.

SET STRETCH GOALS AND TARGETS

Top performers set higher goals and targets, first and foremost. I've practiced this throughout my entire sales career. I've never waited to be told or asked to sell a certain number of cars, products or services. You should always look at the organization's total sales objectives and not just extrapolate your share of the pie based on how many other salespeople are on your team.

To be a successful top performer, you must set higher, more ambitious goals and targets than you're asked to accomplish. Mediocrity is for anyone, but top performers attain higher results by setting bigger goals and targets, formulating their individual sales plan (which we'll discuss in detail in chapter 4) and strategically managing the results accordingly.

Mediocrity is for anyone. To be a successful top performer, you must set higher, more ambitious goals and targets than you're asked to accomplish.

PLAN AND MONITOR OBJECTIVES

The second best practice of top performers is that they break down those big goals and targets, creating a detailed action plan and milestones to help them achieve their entire year's objectives. Top performers always want to know where they stand, and pay attention to the numbers constantly to ensure they stay on track to meet or exceed their goals. They always break the numbers down into yearly, monthly, weekly and daily objectives. Top performers always know where they stand so they can make strategic adjustments to keep pace at all times.

For example, I always use a spreadsheet to keep track of my goals and results for each month and for the year overall. The one I use is very detailed and complex (only a portion of it is shown on the facing page), but you can design something with even a few basic formulas to monitor your own progress against your targets and objectives. We'll revisit a version of this spreadsheet in chapter 6 as well, but for now this excerpt from the larger spreadsheet will simply show you what's possible in terms of tracking your actual results against your goals.

2015 MONTHLY SALES TARGETS			2015 MONTHLY DELIVERY TARGETS			
MONTH	2015 # SALES TARGET	2015 ACTUAL SALES	MONTH	DEALER ASSIGNED TARGET	PERSONAL 2015 DLVRY TRGT	2015 ACTUAL YTD DLV'S
JAN	14	11	JAN	14	14	14
FEB	14	9	FEB	14	14	5
MAR	16	17	MAR	14	13	13
APR	19	14	APR	14	20	14
MAY	18	21	MAY	15	20	23
JUNE	18	16	JUNE	14	17	15
JULY	18	10	JULY	15	17	10
AUG	18	21	AUG	14	17	18
SEPT	18	0	SEPT	14	17	0
OCT	18	0	OCT	14	17	0
NOV	15	0	NOV	14	17	0
DEC	14	0	DEC	14	17	0
targets	200	119	Total	170	200	112
AVG	16.67	14.88	AVG	14.17	16.67	14.00
			DLVD YTD	% of Target	FR GL	
			0	#DIV/0!	0	
		Lex target	112	56.00%	88	
		Avg/ mth	14.00	84.00%		
		SOLD				
	SLS AWAY	DEL'S AWAY				
	-81	-88				

DEFINE THE PURPOSE OF A SALES CALL OR MEETING

The third best practice is about having a clear objective for every call or meeting. We talk about this in sales meetings from time to time but most salespeople just don't get it. Before you pick up the phone or try to engage a client face to face, you must have an action plan.

Have a clearly defined purpose for the call and know the expected outcome:

- Are you calling or following up about a sale or event?
- Are you calling to offer more value or to inform about a change or improvement in the product or service?
- Is there a time-sensitive incentive now available that improves the client's situation and that may increase your chance of closing the deal?
- Are you calling to schedule an appointment or meeting? And what is the desired outcome of that meeting?

BE A GOOD LISTENER

The fourth best practice is listening (as mentioned in the third principle of the previous chapter). Only after you have listened carefully to understand your potential client's point of view and needs, should you be conveying feedback. That's how top performers close more deals and make higher incomes.

You're better off listening your way into making a deal rather than talking your way out of a deal altogether.

High achievers are better informed than the average salesperson about the client's needs and wants because they listen carefully to them; and, therefore, good listeners are better positioned to offer solutions and strategies to fulfill the client's needs. You're better off listening your way into making a deal rather than talking your way out of a deal altogether.

ASK HIGH-VALUE QUESTIONS

Top performers excel at qualifying their prospects. To do that well, you have to ask tough, important, high-value questions. Top performers first listen well to clients to gather information, and then they probe so they can fully uncover their prospects' core issues. (See chapter 7 for a much more detailed discussion of qualifying prospects.)

Take, for example, a recent client who was at the end of their lease; the salesperson they dealt with had already tried to renew their lease earlier, and was now giving it another shot at lease-end but could not get them to commit. The policy at our dealership is that before any final lease returns or buy-outs, I get a final kick at trying to renew the clients. So this particular client met with me and initially simply expressed their desire to go down to one car; in fact, they were so firm in this decision that they had already contacted their insurance company to cancel the insurance effective midnight that day.

Instead of leaving it at that and accepting their decision at face value, I began to ask them a series of probing questions to explore what was really behind their decision not to renew the lease. It turned out that their circumstances and priorities had changed and they thought they could no longer afford two cars, or at least would have to reduce their payments significantly. They clearly laid out for me, in response to my probing questions, all the reasons they did not want or need to renew.

In turn, I proceeded to try and add value for these customers and to find them a different solution by looking at their situation from another angle. Even though they had laid out their concerns and their firm intention to drop off their car that day, they were still sitting in my office. I sensed that if I could make a case that would add value for them, I would have a chance to retain these customers and renew the lease—even though from their perspective they thought they didn't need a second car.

So I laid out all the incentives available to them, including $3,000 in cash, first payment waiver, lower monthly payments than on their previous car, a refund of their original security deposit of $4,500, newer and more useful technology, and an extended warranty that included some maintenance. But the one thing that made the deal fly and wrapped all the value I had proposed together was that, based on all these incentives, I would hand them a check for $6,700, covering almost one year of payments.

The whole value proposition suddenly made sense to them: Get a newer, more fun vehicle *and* get a refund check even bigger than their security deposit, plus an additional loyalty payment to drive away a new car.

This deal was only possible because I asked probing questions to discover what the customers' key issues were; I carefully listened to the responses to understand their real, underlying concerns and priorities; and as a result I was able to propose a solution that truly added value for them.

Sometimes the deal just won't be possible, but not qualifying or probing for the core issues will leave you very little chance of closing more deals.

Getting at what the customer really values and what their priorities and concerns are starts with asking key high-value questions such as these:

- Will you be using the vehicle more for work or routine family needs?
- Is there anything that would keep you from making a decision now?
- What's your current mileage on your present vehicle?

- Are you planning on doing similar mileage or have your circumstances changed?
- What research have you done online and what are the main criteria that must be satisfied?
- Have you thought about an alternative such as . . . ?
- What concerns do you have, if any, about moving forward?
- What made you decide to look at and consider our product?
- Are you familiar with our dealership and our high-value sales philosophy?
- Are you aware of all the additional benefits of doing business with us?
- Are you familiar with, or aware of, all the recent awards, rankings or safety standards of the model you're interested in and how they compare to our competition?

CLARIFY THE ISSUES

Top performers always seek clarity. To accomplish this, they listen intently to the client's point of view and emotions, addressing them only when they are completely clear on the customer's perspective. This involves making a note of key issues or concerns that come up, asking probing questions to clarify them, and addressing them individually to make sure you've covered all the points. This tells the potential client that you've been listening all along and brings a sense of comfort that you're both on the same page and that you have their best interest in mind.

LISTEN FIRST, THEN PRESENT

While having good listening skills and clarifying key issues are essential to making any agreement, the full benefit of these skills is manifested in the seventh best practice: presentation. Top performers wait to present, after making sure they understand the customer's key needs and concerns.

The temptation for many salespeople is to jump in right away and start presenting the product and its features, to cut to the chase and close the deal as quickly as possible. But demonstrating to the client how much product knowledge you have will rarely close the sale if you are elaborating on features that are irrelevant to them, or on points that are less emotionally important to them. Listen first, clarify and then present to address the customer's key concerns.

RECAP THE ISSUES AND ADAPT TO THE SITUATION

Top performers usually tie in the eighth and ninth best practices together as they are directly connected to each other.

The eighth best practice is to recap the important issues before making the presentation. The ninth practice naturally follows from that, as you're adapting the presentation to the situation based on the fact that you've already listened to and clarified the issues (as outlined in best practices four and six).

Adapting to the customer's changing situation or priorities is especially necessary in a long sales cycle that involves many calls and meetings.

Summarizing key issues and adapting your presentation to address them specifically enables you to focus on what's important to your prospects rather than ramble on about less important or irrelevant points. You may need to modify or adapt as you go, due to what you discover about the customer's changing priorities or a change in the customer's situation. This is particularly true in a long sales cycle that might involve multiple calls and meetings.

Focus on what will help to close the deal by addressing those needs in your presentation.

POSITION YOURSELF AGAINST THE COMPETITION

The tenth practice is about knowing how to position your product or service. You can do this effectively, again, by listening and clarifying to know what other products or services the potential customer has been comparing. This sort of feedback allows you to position yourself and your product's features and advantages accordingly, instead of talking to points that do not make the case to buy your product.

By listening actively and carefully to everything the customer is telling you, you may even discern sticking points as they relate to the competition, including features like safety, technology, convenience, cargo room and fuel economy. When you obtain that kind of detailed information by listening and probing, you're better able to position yourself and your product, to close the sale and to make a better deal overall for you and the potential customer.

FOCUS AND PAY ATTENTION

The eleventh practice is simple, so simple it shouldn't even need saying: focus on the client! Don't be distracted by cell phones, other conversations around you, noises or lack of preparation. Focus only on what matters to the client and offer solutions that show them you're giving them the attention they deserve.

TURN OBJECTIONS INTO OPPORTUNITIES

Always be prepared for objections and don't perceive them as problems or roadblocks. Top performers love objections as they pretty much pave the way for you to overcome key issues in order to close the deal. Objections are not negatives; instead, they provide top performers with strategic negotiating points to address, and enable them to strengthen their position and close the deal.

PLAN FOR NEXT STEPS

The thirteenth best practice of top performers is that they always establish next steps. In today's busy environment, decision makers are always on the go, so it's always important to establish next steps while you have the client's attention, or risk losing them for good if you don't. Book follow-up appointments, schedule return calls and establish objectives for next steps, for you and your client.

FOLLOW UP

Following up after the initial meeting is the crucial fourteenth practice, even after you've established next steps. Many sales are lost right here because the average salesperson does not conduct a follow-up call or send a follow-up email.

Following up doesn't have to be a lot of work and could be as simple as an email to confirm next steps, a call to review key details, or to reconfirm an expected outcome. Whatever the reason, following up within twenty-four hours of a sales call or meeting is a must, unless you've agreed on a different timeframe with the prospect.

Many studies publish statistics on sales follow-up and closing ratios, but the one that is most revealing to me is published by the National Sales Executive Association, as follows:

SALES STATISTICS

- 48% of all salespeople never follow up with a prospect.

- 25% of salespeople make only two contacts and stop.

- 12% of salespeople make only three contacts and stop.
- Only 10% of salespeople make more than three contacts.
- 2% of all sales are made on the first contact.
- 3% of sales are made on the second contact.
- 5% of sales are made on the third contact.
- 10% of sales are made on the fourth contact.
- 80% of all sales are made between the fifth and twelfth contact.

The simple fact is that constructive persistence will pay off. Plan and strategize your follow-ups to ensure that you progress through the sales process towards closing the deal. Every time you follow up with a prospect the goal should be more progress towards a yes.

Based on technology today, follow-up communication methods can include email, phone, text, letters, social media and in person. You want to ensure that each contact is progressive, building on your relationship with the client and allowing you to get to, or past, five points of contact—the minimum necessary to close most deals, according to the statistics above. The more follow-up you do with your clients, the more you increase your chances of success.

FILL YOUR PIPELINE

"Always be closing" is a popular maxim in sales; I say you should always be prospecting as well. In order to keep the pipeline flowing and to minimize the highs and lows of sales, top performers set prospecting time aside every week to ensure they stay busy and productive in the long term.

Leads can come from several sources, such as referrals, your existing portfolio, community events, clients you've met recently, sales calls, sending out follow-up letters and emails, social

CUSTOMER CONTACT LIST (CURRENT MONTH)

GUEST ID	EVENT / OCCASION	GUEST NAME	SOURCE	DATE	CM	MODEL	
1		Vladimir	Sales Call	30-Sep-14	Y	11 RX350	
2		Marisa	Lse Rnw	4-Oct-14	Y	15 RX350	
3		Melissa	Nx Prev	30-Sep-14	Y	11 RX350	
4		David and Sherri	Repeat	30-Sep-14	Y	15 GS350	
5		Anne	Walk In	30-Sep-14	Y	15 IS250	
6		Paul	Walk In	30-Sep-14	Y	11 RX350	
7		Ken	Sales Call	30-Sep-14	Y	ES/RX	
8		Brian	Sales Call	2-Oct-14	Y	11 4RUNNER	
9		Peter	BB	2-Oct-14	Y	13 RX350	
10	SALE	Maureen	Repeat	2-Oct-14	Y	15 RX350	
11		Robert	Lse Rnw	1-Oct-14	Y	15 RX350	
12		Andrew	Lse Rnw	1-Oct-14		15 GX460	
13		Abdel	Walk In	3-Oct-14		14 ES300h	
14		Vlad	Lse Rnw	30-Sep-14		15 LS430	
15		Marisa and Steve	Lse Rnw	4-Oct-14	Y	14 IS250	
16	SALE	Martha	Walk In	25-Oct-14		15 RX350	
17		Phan	Walk In	25-Oct-14		15 RX350	
18	SALE	Sathy	Walk In	25-Oct-14		15 CT200h	
19		Cindy	Referral	27-Oct-14		15 RX350	
20		Jason And Evlyne	Walk In	27-Oct-14		NX200t	
21		Lori	Sales Call	28-Oct-14		RX450h	
22		Rose	Walk In	28-Oct-14		NX200t	
23		GARY	Walk In	28-Oct-14		ES350	
24		GLENN	SALES CALL	28-Oct-14		IS250	
25		CHARLES	Repeat	30-Oct-14		CT300h	
26		RICK	SALES CALL	30-Oct-14		GS350AWD	
27		Andrea	Repeat	30-Oct-14		RX350	

The closing ratio of 0.40 (top right) was calculated on a larger version of this spreadsheet with a larger sample size of forty-seven customer contacts and actual results of nineteen vehicles sold.

Closing Ratio: 0.40

PHONE NUMBER	EMAIL ADDRESS	NOTES	RESULT
(555) 416-1234	aaawdfan@gmail.com	call to confirm apt.LM 10/1/14	SOLD
(555) 416-1234	aaawdfan@gmail.com	Apt Set In Calendar.	SOLD
(555) 416-1234	aaawdfan@gmail.com	still want Trg 11 RX	
(555) 416-1234	aaawdfan@gmail.com	waiting for GS pricing	SOLD
(555) 416-1234	aaawdfan@gmail.com	emailed twice to follow up	
(555) 416-1234	aaawdfan@gmail.com	Apt Set In Calendar.	SOLD
(555) 416-1234	aaawdfan@gmail.com	Cld to Sch TD. LM 10/11	APT
(555) 416-1234	aaawdfan@gmail.com	Fr sales CL	SOLD
(555) 416-1234	aaawdfan@gmail.com	BB	APT
(555) 416-1234	aaawdfan@gmail.com	Repeat	SOLD
(555) 416-1234	aaawdfan@gmail.com	had accdt. Need car asap. Lm 10/2	SOLD
(555) 416-1234	aaawdfan@gmail.com	Wants GX instd of GX.	
(555) 416-1234	aaawdfan@gmail.com	wants price on 14ES300h.	
(555) 416-1234	aaawdfan@gmail.com	LSE Buy out. Second car.	
(555) 416-1234	aaawdfan@gmail.com	Apt Set In Calendar.	SOLD
(555) 416-1234	aaawdfan@gmail.com	COMP with x3	SOLD
(555) 416-1234	aaawdfan@gmail.com	decide on tues	APT
(555) 416-1234	aaawdfan@gmail.com	walk in SOLD	SOLD
(555) 416-1234	aaawdfan@gmail.com	spoke to guest. Want exclusive price	
(555) 416-1234	aaawdfan@gmail.com	call when NX comes in.	
(555) 416-1234	aaawdfan@gmail.com		APT
(555) 416-1234	aaawdfan@gmail.com	FOLLOW UP WITH NX PRICING	
(555) 416-1234	aaawdfan@gmail.com	Cash deal with wife. Away till Mon.	
(555) 416-1234	aaawdfan@gmail.com		APT
(555) 416-1234	aaawdfan@gmail.com		
(555) 416-1234	aaawdfan@gmail.com	Notify about private sale.	
(555) 416-1234	aaawdfan@gmail.com	walk in SOLD	SOLD

media, etc. In the next chapter, we will explore prospecting methods in more detail to help you build and grow your consistent
client base.

In October 2014, I decided to conduct a more detailed study
of all the clients I had contact with to determine the effect of a
more concerted prospecting effort. The following chart shows the
actual results of that study.

DEAL WITH DECISION MAKERS

Top sales performers know that closing a deal requires dealing
with a decision maker. They don't waste time seeking middlemen
or front-line gatekeepers. They always find a way to the source to
get a decision.

For example, during the period of 2004-11 while running a
marketing company, I often got involved with training the tele-
marketers in charge of scheduling appointments. These calls
mostly consisted of warm calls, as we were referred to many of
these prospects by a reputable local real estate company and were
able to tell people that when we called them. Others were colder
calls, however, made to potential clients who were only vague-
ly familiar with the local real estate company by name. In the
case of the cold calls, there was almost always a gatekeeper, as
we would be calling many professional services offices, such as
lawyers, insurance companies and mortgage companies. In some
cases we would have a direct contact name, but in others we
would have to source the correct contact through the reception-
ist, assistant or whoever answered the phone.

I taught the staff making the calls that one of the most effective ways of getting past the gatekeeper was always to assertively
and confidently ask for the decision maker or contact directly by
name if available:

- "Good morning! This is Everold Reid calling for Mr. Jones," or, "Good morning, this is Everold Reid. Please put me through to Mr. Jones," worked a lot better than, "This is Everold Reid. Can I speak to Mr. Jones?" or, "Is Mr. Jones available?" The direct, bold approach usually gave the impression that the decision maker was expecting the call or may have had prior contact with the person calling him and was aware of the purpose of the call. Your assertive tone conveys more confidence to the gatekeeper, thus reducing the chances of screening. If the contact's name is unknown, use the same bold approach, but ask for the individual you are seeking by their title.

- In the case of a face-to-face meeting, a top performer would likely show up to an appointment and say, "Good morning, I'm Everold Reid, here for a 10:00 a.m. appointment with Mr. Jones," instead of asking if Mr. Jones is in or saying, "My name is Everold Reid; I'm here to see Mr. Jones." I've seen the effect of the more timid approach almost daily, when visitors arrive at our dealership for various meetings and are kept waiting because they weren't assertive enough or specific enough. They are asked many more questions than needed, and sometimes the message to the decision maker is watered down to the point of uncertainty about who's visiting. The direct approach will show preparation, and lead to clarity when arriving for the appointment.

TREAT THE GATEKEEPER WITH RESPECT

If you do have to go through a gatekeeper to get to the real decision maker, that front-line person can be your ally, or a major obstacle to getting to the decision maker. The end result is usually up to you and how you conduct yourself in dealing with the gate-keeper, especially when you're attempting a sales call without the benefit of a direct contact name. In that case, you need to get the gatekeeper on your side within the first thirty seconds. You can do that by complimenting their professionalism and thanking them for their assistance, for starters.

When attempting a call without a contact name, one approach is to ask for the decision maker by their title or in relation to the department they are in charge of. You can also gently probe the gatekeeper on the basis of needing to send out an important email or details relating to that department, and say that you're verifying it gets to the right person.

You can also politely and directly ask who's in charge of fleet purchasing or budgeting, for example, if you are reaching out to larger companies for potential new accounts. Don't forget to ask for the best times to reach the contact person, and for additional contact details such as email and cell when possible.

Always be polite and appreciative; treating the gatekeeper with respect and courtesy will usually go a long way to getting to the person or information you are seeking. And never make a pitch directly to the gatekeeper, or accept a no or negative decision from someone who's not authorized to say yes.

KEEP IN TOUCH

Top performers keep in touch with their clients or prospects. They always dedicate daily, weekly or monthly time to follow up, ask for referrals and to check in on how things are going. It's about keeping yourself in the back of their minds so that any thought of your product or service will serve as a reminder to contact only you.

BE A TRENDSETTER

Being a top performer means doing things better than most of your peers or co-workers. Top performers set trends and take initiative that co-workers and others follow. They lead by creative, results-oriented examples. It's easier to lead after you've demonstrated results. Top performers provide creative ideas for others, and make others around them better.

It's easier to lead after you've demonstrated results.

MANAGE YOURSELF

Autonomy is a key characteristic of top performers in the workplace. Of course, even a top performer will more than likely have a manager to report to and to whom they're accountable, but for the most part they require little or no supervision. High-performance employees manage their time well, complete their workload and learn from their experience to plan ahead with a great deal of autonomy.

Top performers usually have more flexibility than typical performers, simply because they achieve above-average results and lead by example. Average performers have little or no autonomy, and are usually closely monitored by supervisors. Top performers rely on their own strengths and insights to get the job done.

NETWORK, NETWORK, NETWORK

Top performers are people-oriented and possess strong networking and relationship-building skills. High performers are confident in reaching out to others within the organization they represent, as well as turning to outside sources to gather information, thus they contribute ample knowledge to the organization.

Networking not only allows you to gain new customers, but it can also help you to gain new ideas and to improve yourself in many areas. Top performers have larger networks than the average worker, a broad social and professional group that they can contact for different resources whenever the need arises. This ability to collaborate with others provides growth for the high-performance employee and benefits the entire company or organization.

BE OPEN-MINDED

A top performer usually is level headed and keeps cool under pressure. They are emotionally stable and consistent in their style of work and leadership. They will compromise and be open-minded, and will change their position when the time is right instead of being stubborn or confrontational. This trait helps top performers learn quickly and become excellent problem solvers.

To this point, *The Reid Method* has outlined the general characteristics for sales success. From here on, we'll get into much more detail about some of the key points we've introduced and provide you with how-to advice and strategies for putting these best practices to work.

Chapters 4 and 5, up next, are at the core of *The Reid Method*: creating a sales action plan and a marketing plan are essential components for high-performance sales success.

SUMMARY

- **Set stretch goals and targets:** Mediocrity is for anyone, but top performers attain higher results by setting bigger goals and targets, formulating their individual sales plan and strategically managing their results accordingly.

- **Plan ahead and track performance to be successful:** Top performers always want to know where they stand and pay attention to the numbers constantly to ensure they stay on track to meet or exceed their goals.

- **Set objectives:** Before you pick up the phone or try to engage a client face to face you must have a plan for the interaction. Outline your objectives before engaging with clients.

- **Listen carefully:** Top performers listen attentively to their clients so they can offer the best solutions and strategies to fulfill the client's needs. You're better off listening your way into making a deal rather than talking your way out of a deal altogether.

- **Ask high-value questions:** Top performers not only listen well to clients to gather information, they also uncover their prospects' core issues by asking high-value, probing questions.

- **Clarify the issues:** Top performers listen intently to understand fully the client's point of view and emotions before jumping in to address them or make a sales pitch. Clarifying what the potential client is telling you shows him or her that you've been listening all along, and brings a sense of comfort that you're both on the same page.

- **Wait to present:** Top performers wait to present after making sure they understand the key needs and concerns. No sense elaborating on irrelevant points. Listen first, clarify and then present to address key concerns.

- **Open with a recap:** Recap the important issues and concerns before making the actual presentation.

- **Adapt your presentation to the situation:** Focus on what's important to your prospects rather than ramble on about less important or irrelevant points.

- **Know how to position your product properly:** Know what other products or services the potential customer has been comparing. This feedback allows you to position yourself and your product's features and advantages accordingly.

- **Focus on the prospect:** Don't be distracted by cell phones, other conversations, noises or lack of preparation. Focus only on what matters to the client and offer solutions that show them you're giving them the attention they deserve.

- **Be prepared for objections:** Objections are not negatives; rather, they provide top performers with strategic negotiating points to address and help strengthen their position to close the deal.

- **Always establish next steps:** Book follow-up appointments, schedule return calls and establish objectives for next steps—or risk losing your prospect forever.

- **Follow up after the call or meeting:** This could involve a confirmation of next steps, review of details, or reconfirming an expected outcome. Following up within twenty-four hours is a must, unless you've agreed on a different timeframe with the prospect.

- **Prospect continuously to keep the pipeline flowing:** In order to keep the pipeline flowing and to minimize the highs and lows of sales, top performers set prospecting time aside every week to ensure they stay busy and productive. Always find creative ways to keep prospecting, at work and socially.

- **Deal with decision makers:** Top performers don't waste time seeking middlemen or front-line gatekeepers. They always find ways to the source to get a decision.

- **Keep in touch with customers:** Top performers dedicate daily, weekly or monthly time to follow up with clients, ask for referrals and to check in on how things are going. They become the go-to contact for clients, always keeping front-of-mind.

- **Be a good role model and lead by example:** Top performers set trends and take initiative that co-workers and others follow. They lead by example, and by being creative and results-oriented.

- **Take control, lead and earn autonomy:** High-performing team members usually have more flexibility than typical performers simply because they achieve above-average results and lead by example.

- **Network relentlessly:** Top performers have larger networks than the average worker, people they can contact as resources whenever the need arises. This ability to collaborate with others provides growth for the high-performance employee and benefits the entire company or organization.

- **Always have an open mind:** Top performers will compromise and be open-minded when the time is right; they'll change their position instead of being stubborn or confrontational.

CHAPTER 4

THE ACTION PLAN
Create Your Own Sales and Marketing Blueprint

So, you've decided to elevate your sales game—that's great! But before you jump in with both feet, there are some key elements to put in place that are critical to your success. Even if you're prepared and follow best practices, there will always be things that you can control (like your attitude and determination) and others that you can't (such as the overall leadership of a dealership or sales organization, or market trends).

Even though you may not always be in control, you can exert influence. If you've got a positive attitude and have ambitious goals and ideas, I encourage you to share them or seek permission to try them on your own. Dealerships are always looking for sharp, creative minds with good ideas to improve the way they are doing things, and to separate themselves from the competition. Don't be afraid to suggest or share your positive ideas.

To set yourself up for success in sales and to implement your great ideas, you should at least create a basic sales and marketing action plan. It should include having a thorough conversation with your sales manager and colleagues about expectations, goals, sales targets and how you plan to achieve those goals through your marketing plans and efforts.

YOUR INDIVIDUAL SALES PLAN

A sales plan is a crucial tool for all salespeople, but few salespeople have or use one. I usually hear from my colleagues that their goal is to sell as much as they can, but that's not a goal.

> A sales plan is a crucial tool for all salespeople, but few salespeople have or use one.

Your company should have a sales plan, and, if that's the case, you should definitely make a point of learning and following it. And even if your company does have an overall sales plan in place, if you don't have an individual sales plan as well, you're missing an opportunity to succeed.

Setting Sales Goals and Targets

Your individual sales plan is based on your personal goals, not just the sales target that is handed out to you by your manager as your piece of the overall dealership's pie. For example, in calendar year 2015, my dealership's overall target is about 1,100 new and pre-owned deliveries. With an average of eight salespeople, that means that each sales rep should sell about 137 vehicles each, on average. The target I was assigned for 2015 by the dealership was 170, the highest of all, based on my years of experience and past sales record; but my personal target was 200.

My personal target was based on my own personal goal for the level of income I wanted to achieve during the year, as well as on the sales numbers I felt I could achieve based on my ability and drive. I am not satisfied with being just one of the pack, selling the average of 137 vehicles for the year. The fact that I was assigned a target of 170 by management speaks to the confidence of the dealership in my abilities, which further adds to my drive to achieve a higher target, and the pride I would feel in exceeding what I'm asked to do.

As illustrated in chapter 3 under Plan and Monitor Objectives, not only do I monitor and reference my sales targets and personal income goals constantly to stay focused on my objectives and progress, but I also create a personal sales plan to help me actually achieve those goals. No matter what targets you have been handed or may have set for yourself, I strongly recommend that you create your own personal sales plan to help you achieve them. Your sales plan will serve as a constant reference point that will help to keep you motivated and focused.

Your sales plan should be short, simple and to the point, and it should start with your sales forecast or sales target. Then you need to create a detailed breakdown of the forecast—of the sales goals you plan to achieve by month, annually, by customer count and by product.

Developing Sales Strategies and Tactics

Your sales plan should also include two other major components: the sales strategy (the overall plan necessary to accomplish your goals) and sales tactics (the specific actions and steps needed to execute the plan). A sales strategy might be to let the people in your community know about your company's history of community involvement, while the associated tactics might include attending chamber of commerce meetings, placing ads in the local papers or on radio, hosting an event at your place of business, or launching a direct mail campaign.

A sales plan is basically your own strategic and tactical blueprint for achieving or exceeding your sales quotas, with all types of clients; therefore, your personal sales plan should include

strategies and tactics for acquiring new business, as well as growing your existing book of business (we'll look at strategies for
both these categories of customers a little later in the chapter).

> Your personal sales plan should include strategies
> and tactics for acquiring new business, as well as
> growing your existing book of business.

When developing your sales plan, it is important to link it with
your individual marketing plan so that they support each other,
and to set out in detail how you will deliver marketing objectives,
reach your target market segments, and support major marketing
activities, such as promotional drives. For example, which target
markets are you aiming for and what is the timeline? (We'll take
a much more detailed look at marketing plans and strategies later
in this chapter and in chapter 5.)

An Example of a Sales Plan in Action

For example, part of my sales plan to hit my overall 2015 sales forecast was to sell a certain number of a new 2016 model, a significant
redesign of the product with a major launch planned to reintroduce
it. Rather than simply waiting for the corporate marketing campaign to drive people in to the showroom to see this new model, I
developed my own marketing plan to help me sell the quantity of
this new product I'd set as a goal for myself. In fact, I developed my
own personal marketing strategy to help me achieve my personal
sales goals for this product—in advance of the launch.

I wanted to engage our client base four to six months ahead
of the actual launch date for the new model to ramp up interest
and to obtain pre-orders for this new vehicle. From our existing
database, we selected clients who were currently driving similar models and would potentially have an interest in the new
product. I chose to reach them by using an e-blast as a teaser

promotion, including in the message a pdf or jpg e-flyer with elegant imaging, scripts and links to the new redesign on the corporate website. The emphasis was on the vehicle's new look, advanced technology and the opportunity to be among the first to pre-order and own one.

My sales goal was to line up pre-orders ahead of the launch, so that when the new model was actually released and available, I would have my personal order bank. Using this kind of marketing to support your sales plan is an effective way of having orders and inquiries coming to you even while you're sleeping.

Whatever your specific sales plan may be, you should always try to build a plan that includes strategies and tactics that, when executed, produce results that outperform your expectations. Be ambitious, be bold: Setting yourself stretch targets in your sales plan and developing marketing plans to get you there will translate into sales results that might just surprise everyone—including you!

ASSESS THE SITUATION

Before you set out to reinvent the wheel and to start or improve on a personal sales and marketing plan, it's most important to assess the current situation to know what you already have, if anything, as a foundation from which to build. Then develop a strategy for achieving your sales plan, and follow that by identifying specific tactics that will enable you to deliver the results you are looking for. Implementing a well thought out, comprehensive sales plan in this way will differentiate you from most salespeople out there, who just jump into selling without any concerted plan.

For example, over the last three years, I sold and leased close to 600 retail high-end vehicles by first having my personal sales goal of about 200 retail deliveries per year (as I pointed out before, this personal goal was above the number the dealership handed me as a sales target). I would not have achieved these results by waiting for floor traffic, and that's just not my style anyway. Instead, I proactively went after the business, first assessing the current situation and opportunities before creating my marketing plan. I identified that the dealership had a huge, untapped lease and finance portfolio that was shrinking rapidly due to lack of attention and no substantive retention plan.

I first assessed what was available from which to build—a database of thousands of virtually untapped lease and finance customers—and identified a strategy to mine this database for new business. I remember asking management for some contacts from the database and did not receive them for months. This delay turned out to be a big financial loss for me individually and for the dealership, as many clients simply returned their vehicles at lease-end and we lost them to competitors due to inconsistent contact from the dealership, or a complete lack of it.

As a tactic to implement the strategy—to stop that trend of our customers walking away at lease-end—I chose to use a contact-management tool that was already available at the dealership. This allowed me to create letter templates that could be uploaded directly to an existing mail-merge software, personalizing all the letters to create a very low-cost direct marketing piece. This was a multimillion dollar software product that was sitting on every salesperson's computer and not being utilized to a fraction of its capabilities. I decided to put it to good use to help retain customers and generate new business.

Although I had no formal training on this software, I made a point of seeking help to understand it well enough so that I could target active and qualified leads. I had identified its potential and I took the necessary action to have it work for me. I sent out these marketing letters about three to four times annually, and the response became very consistent and predictable, with a closing rate of about fifteen percent every time. Clients would diligently follow the instructions to call and book an appointment for us to meet, evaluate their situation and to see what we could offer to improve it.

This example shows that we developed both strategy and tactics in our sales plan after taking time to assess the current situation. That assessment revealed not only that we had an untapped database of clients we were losing and could convert to more sales, but also that we had the software tools already available to help us manage these contacts—all we had to do was use them. The strategy was to reach our existing portfolio of clients and offer early renewals or upgrades. The tactic was to offer incentives, such as lower interest rates, cash incentives and payments waivers, potential lower payments and/or additional features of newer models. Putting all the components of the sales plan together in this way translated into tangible results, for me and for the dealership.

The marketing letter had a clear, concise proposition, offering clients the option to upgrade their current vehicle to a newer, more advanced model (thus updating their auto needs as their personal situation may have changed), or offering a financial benefit such as reduced payments and cash incentives. The results were measurable and predictable; for every one hundred letters that I mailed out, I could count on approximately thirty percent to turn into calls and appointments, and about a fifteen percent closing ratio depending on the sales tactic used. Based on these consistently good results, we established a quarterly direct mail campaign for the entire dealership, which became part of our annual marketing plan and strategy.

Know your marketplace and identify the marketing tools you already have available.

All sales action plans need to consider the customers' needs and characteristics, including what type of products they want and what level of service they expect. It's essential to know when, where and how your customers buy, and the key factors influencing their buying decisions. Know your marketplace and identify the tools you already have available. I knew that in our high-income, predominantly middle- to upper-class marketplace, our clientele were keen on changing vehicles often and so this early renewal campaign was a perfect fit. Market trends and general competition are also important factors to consider in your action plan.

SALES STRATEGIES AND TACTICS FOR NEW AND EXISTING CUSTOMERS

As we discussed above, your sales plan should include strategies for two main classes of customers: one for existing customers, and another for new business acquisition, or conquest business, as it's referred to in the automotive sales world.

Strategies and Tactics for New Business

Your new business acquisition plan should include at least four strategies with associated tactics, all designed to capture new customers and grow market share. Whether as an individual or a sales team looking to increase sales, you must plan, outline and share your new business acquisition plan to have the entire sales team onboard, and for the entire team to be successful. Following are some examples of strategies and tactics you might consider incorporating into your own plan.

- **Strategy:** Exceed your sales quota. The associated tactics could be making no less than twenty sales calls per day, sending out 100 direct mail pieces each month or creating at least fifteen proposals each week. The key here is to know your prospect ratio: How many contacts are needed to ultimately achieve your sales quota?

- **Strategy:** Increase marketplace awareness of your products and services. The associated tactic could be becoming a member of two or three professional associations or organizations that best represent your client base or demographic, such as BIA groups, local chamber business groups and organized networking groups. I would also recommend attending conventions, business trade shows or fairs that your potential customers attend, such as a Marque d'Elegance luxury supercar event. Use social media to announce your own upcoming events, such as sales promotions, community days, service specials, new product updates and new model launches.

- **Strategy:** Increase community awareness of products and services. Another effective way to meet and network with people is simply by volunteering and giving back; so the associated tactic may include becoming a volunteer with one to three community organizations, such as the local hospital, a church, a fundraising event, service club or other charitable organization.

- **Strategy:** Always seek to obtain referrals. One tactic might be, at delivery or within a week of delivering your product or service (while your new client is most excited), to ask for the names and numbers of at least three friends, family or associates they personally know who may have a need for your products or services. Another good time to request referrals is after sending or giving a thank-you gift to your new, excited client. You can also request referrals at service calls, or at business functions or events attended by any of your satisfied clients.

Strategies and Tactics for Existing Customers

We spoke earlier about your sales plan including strategies and
tactics for building both new and existing business. It's extremely important not to neglect your existing clients. They are
the most predisposed of anyone to do business with you and
some of your most satisfied customers may even become your
raving fans if you take proper care of them and maintain regular
contact.

It is a well known fact in business of any kind that it is much
less costly to retain an existing client than to acquire a new one,
so nurturing your existing customer base is an important, and
potentially more profitable, part of your sales plan. Here are some
effective strategies and tactics to maximize business from your
existing customer base.

- **Strategy:** Develop a keep-in-touch system for yourself.
  Associated tactics could include contacting your existing
  customer base regularly (every month or every three or
  six months depending on your business) to offer new,
  improved ideas that they won't get elsewhere (e.g., improved service systems and added-value propositions).
  Some of my colleagues communicate with their customers
  on blogs, Facebook and Twitter; others use traditional
  channels such as newsletters and direct mail campaigns
  to provide valued-added information and to solicit leads
  from them. This kind of ongoing communication might
  include tips on winter driving, specials on winter tires,
  other seasonal recommendations and specials, new product announcements and contests.

- **Strategy:** Seek prospects from within your immediate customer base. In the automotive world of sales and service
  this is the easiest tactic to use. In the auto sales world

you always hear the saying, "Sales sells the first car and service sells the second and more."

Every day, service clients wander throughout showrooms and on lots while waiting for their vehicles to be serviced. Engage these clients, especially those who drive older models and who may be paying high repair bills; offer solutions to convert them to new products easily by presenting value scenarios.

Another tactic can be checking your contact management (CM) programs daily to see which existing customers are scheduled for service, and then be proactive: Greet them and ask them to update you on their current status. This is an easy way to keep in touch and request referrals.

TRACKING YOUR PROGRESS WITH SALES METRICS

Having a detailed sales plan and tracking your progress against it gives you strategic control of your own destiny week to week, and it allows you to remain in control in the long term instead of winging it and playing catch up.

Timeline of Sales Plan

To be successful, every sales and marketing plan must include a detailed timeline to achieve each tactic set forth. This timeline should be broken down at least weekly and monitored daily to make sure you're on track. The sales plan and timeline should be at your fingertips so you can revise it as needed, and to keep track of your progress.

Closing and Prospect Ratio

Only a percentage of the people you reach out to via emails, calls or direct mailers will respond to your marketing efforts and become actual prospects. And only a percentage of those prospects will convert to actual customers. Therefore, it is critical to be aware of and track these ratios to be effective. You need to know how many prospects you need to contact via the various tactics in your plan in order to close the sales you ultimately need.

You should know your prospect and closing ratios based on how many out of every ten leads convert to customers, and ultimately per every one hundred. If you don't know your prospect and closing ratios, you should immediately select a test period to research them. The benchmark ratios may vary by industry but are essential to all.

Start by monitoring your own prospecting and sales activity daily, for a month. How many prospects are you attracting each day from all sources? What percentage of those prospects are you converting each day for a total of closed sales at the end of a sales month?

Calculating Your Prospect and Closing Ratio

The first step is to establish target ratios by monitoring your own prospecting and sales activities for a month (or whatever period that may be appropriate to your industry). Follow these simple steps:

1. After contacting 100 potential customers by phone, email, mailings, in person or by any prospecting means, how many (what percentage) of prospects would result _____?

2. How many (what percentage) could be identified as hot leads_____?

3. How many (what percentage) would you close actual sales with_____?

4. Next, calculate your ratio by dividing the result in (3) by 100 to get your percentage closing ratio_____.

Example: Take 100 potential customers in total. You identify 68 of them (or 68%) as good prospects, of the 68 you identify 47 (or 47% of the total prospect base) as hot leads. Finally, of the 47 hot leads you actually close 25 sales. Your actual closing percentage (or ratio) over that period of time is 25%, that is, 25 of the 100 initial prospects converted to sales.

Identifying 100 Potential Prospects

Note that in the automobile sales world, most dealerships have in place a contact management (CM) system that keeps track of potential clients, mainly those who walk through the doors, are on the lot browsing, or who are reached via telephone sales calls and Internet leads. These types of leads are supplied by the dealerships and all count towards your 100 potentials.

Your remaining prospects should come directly from investing your own time in sourcing leads. As we've discussed earlier, that could be through referrals from existing clients, friends and family; community events and involvement; or your own direct marketing initiatives via direct mailings and social media. More and more these days, sales organizations are driving even greater productivity and higher conversion rates through social selling. You should embrace social media more seriously as an essential part of generating high-quality leads in your overall prospect count. In the next chapter we'll look in more detail at social media and other marketing channels.

YOUR PERSONAL MARKETING PLAN

Every sales plan needs to be supported by a corresponding marketing plan to be effective. Your marketing plan outlines the strategies, tactics and promotions that will help you to achieve your sales targets. We'll look at specific marketing methods in more detail in chapter 5; for now, let's stick to the more general priciples of marketing.

Your marketing strategies could include being active on social media (such as starting or using your own Facebook or LinkedIn page), publishing a monthly or quarterly newsletter, and advertising in local community magazines or papers. You should offer a basic referral fee to your family and friends to encourage them to refer business to you and help to grow your network. Most dealerships or sales companies will pay at least half the referral fee for any deals closed, so take full advantage of those marketing dollars.

Community involvement will provide you many opportunities to give back and to meet lots of potential clients while serving others. The bottom line here is to do anything you can to build your own portfolio of potential clients; don't just wait for sales calls or prospects to walk through the door.

At social or community gatherings, hand out business cards and collect contact details from everyone you meet who could be a potential client. Don't judge—you never know who will refer someone to you. Make many contacts and spread your message. Don't ever stop building your base; your personal network can become your eyes and ears for referrals, and can help to spread the word even while you sleep.

To keep engaged with your contacts and potential clients, send out messages about specials, events, new model introductions or launches, and post these important updates through social media as well. Don't bombard them; rather, be strategic and creative with offerings and incentives, giving them a call to action whenever possible.

It's important to remember that some jurisdictions are putting restrictions on outbound email marketing to protect the privacy of individuals. In Canada, for example, as of July 1, 2014, new legislation prohibits businesses or individuals working with any company from emailing clients without express written consent from them, unless the client has done direct business with the company within the past two years. Be certain that your email strategies are within guidelines. You should familiarize yourself with your local anti-spam laws to ensure that you are in compliance. Both you and your company could face stiff financial penalties if you're convicted of violating these strict anti-spam and other privacy laws.

There are several ways you can be proactive about obtaining consent and being compliant with anti-spam and privacy laws. Some of the common ones in the retail sales environment, such as an auto dealership, would include the following:

- If the client has visited your showroom: Have a basic compliance sheet available, stating the law, the reasons you're gathering the information and how it may be used. The client can then fill in basic contact details, including their email address, phone numbers etc., and sign the sheet right there, giving you permission to communicate in the future when you are trying to negotiate a deal.

- If the client has initiated contact and requests information: If the client has contacted you by phone, it is best to provide them with your email address as well so that they can also initiate the request for further details in writing, via email. This then satisfies the legal requirements for consent and enables you to contact them in the future without having them sign a consent form. However, once that same client visits the showroom in person, you should also get their written consent to keep on file.

One way to engage your new contacts and potential clients for marketing purposes is to set up call-to-action campaigns whereby they have to click through to respond to your offer, and you obtain measurable results, feedback and details for future use.

For example:

- Schedule a no-obligation evaluation or appraisal today and get a $50 gas card just for coming in.
- Call or email to schedule your test drive today and enter a draw for a $100 pre-paid card or gift.

You may have many more creative ideas, but the key is to engage your clients consistently with value-added propositions to see how they respond and what works best for you. In our local trading area, we choose to use various methods of engagement for marketing, including digital boards, movie theatre ads, trendy magazines, online, radio, direct marketing, local community events, and sometimes other mediums that require customer feedback.

Each market is different, so engaging with and getting to know your potential clients as part of your qualifying and selling process helps you to understand trends and characteristics as well as where and how to best target your marketing efforts. There's a lot more information on marketing strategies in chapter 5. For now let's just say, never stop learning about and studying your marketplace.

SUMMARY

- **Create a sales action plan:** Your plan should include having a thorough conversation with your sales manager and colleagues about expectations, goals, sales targets and how you plan to achieve those goals with the support of your marketing plans and efforts.

- **Create and use a simple sales plan:** A working sales plan is a crucial tool for all salespeople or any retail organization. Even though your company may have a sales plan in place, if you don't have an individual sales plan as well, you're missing an opportunity to succeed. Your sales action plan should include a sales forecast and should cover two other major components: sales strategies and sales tactics.

- **Contact Management (CM):** Use a contact management tool to record and track your prospecting and follow-up activities with clients. It's impossible for you to keep track of all the details of each client. A good CM tool will prompt you with a daily work plan; enter all your prospects diligently and the CM tool will do the rest.

- **Strategic approach:** To develop and build a viable, consistent customer base, you should have two main sales strategies: one for existing customers, and the other for new business acquisition.

- **The numbers and results matter:** Keep track of your numbers: prospects, sales, deliveries, average dollars per deal. You can be as elaborate as you want, but a simple tracking system can tell you a lot about your progress.

- **Community involvement:** The key to your sales success is to build your own portfolio of potential clients and not just wait for potential business coming through the door or from sales calls. Community involvement is just one proven way of building a customer base.

- **Use social media to your advantage:** Send out or post important updates or messages about specials, events or new model launches using social media sites to keep engaged with your new contacts, potential clients and existing client base. Keep in mind that sales are increasingly being driven by higher rates of social engagement and conversations in social media.

- **Be aware of and play by the rules:** Be certain that your emailing strategies comply with ethical guidelines and local anti-spam laws. Check how rules on emailing, spam and confidentiality apply in your specific market.

- **Utilize call-to-action campaigns:** Engage new and potential clients by setting up call-to-action campaigns soliciting click-throughs to get measurable results, feedback and to gather valuable stats for future marketing use.

- **Get to know your marketplace:** It's essential to know when, where and how your customers buy and what the key factors influencing their buying decisions are. Make it a priority to know your marketplace, identify the tools you already have available and continue to explore effective ways to target potential customers.

CHAPTER 5

MARKETING STRATEGIES TO BUILD YOUR BUSINESS

Naturally, effective marketing, advertising and promotion are critical to building your business, but there's also more to attracting and retaining customers than inbound or outbound marketing. At the very foundation of business success are a couple of other important principles: leadership and innovation.

But before looking in detail at the range of strategies necessary for success in today's ultra-competitive environment, let's take a look at how business-building strategies have evolved over the years.

THAT WAS THEN . . .

Prior to the rise of the Internet in the mid-1990s, there were four traditional marketing and advertising avenues to build business in the automotive and retail sales industries:

- walk-in or drive-by traffic, depending on location
- print media, including newspapers, flyers and magazines

- electronic media, primarily radio and television
- outdoor signs, such as billboards, bus stop signs or mobile signage, including busses

This was a time when you always heard the phrase, location, location, location. Brand-name dealerships, used-car dealerships and retail outlets with prime, high-traffic and highly visible locations often thrived due to a higher rate of customer traffic flow. Even those with less desirable brands and models would often succeed, because their locations offered optimum exposure, conveniently displaying both new and pre-owned inventory to attract potential buyers passing by.

Plentiful inventory displayed on dealer lots with colorful flags and signs grabbed the attention of many potential clients. This was basic, cost-effective advertising that could generate sales results and last for months and years.

Before the rise of the Internet in the 1990s, a salesperson would be most effective by keeping his or her eyes peeled on traffic, looking for potential clients driving by or wandering on to the lot, or listening for sales calls on the dealership's paging systems. These were the two main ways a potential sale would make its way into dealerships or retail organizations.

Some dealerships, from the 1980s through to the turn of the millennium, had designated salespeople who focused primarily on one specific department: either new or pre-owned vehicles. These salespeople took overflow from the other department only when necessary. This was because the primary source of traffic was walk-ins or incoming sales calls, and sales managers would manage the structure and rotation to be fair to all salespeople, while ensuring proper floor coverage.

Experienced sales agents would want to sell more pre-owned, especially if the dealership had good inventory and location, because commissions were often much higher than on new vehicles. Dealerships also wanted this because they, too, knew where the higher profit margin was, and pre-owned vehicle sales also brought additional profits to their service departments. For this reason, they would have good closers assigned to the used-car department to take care of those clients.

In the mid-1980s, a new trend in automotive marketing became more prominent, with the introduction of auto malls. This retail business model offers multiple brands in a central, highly visible location, where clients can conveniently shop and compare.

The auto-mall concept enables comparisons and offers convenience, similar to the Internet today, where detailed comparisons can be made online before a client even ventures out to look at or test drive products.

Auto malls started popping up more frequently across North America as dealers quickly realized significant advantages in high retail visibility, more strength in numbers by sharing land costs, and concentrated advertising and marketing efforts through auto-mall associations and groups.

Before the rise of the Internet, the primary sources of business were walk-in traffic and incoming sales calls.

The auto-mall retail model and marketing concept continues to be successful, because any type of convenience for potential clients is added value in today's hyperactive environment, and auto malls attract clients by offering greater selection than a stand-alone dealership. Ultimately, the primary goals of the dealers are to source new customers, to maintain existing clients, and to build a solid customer base for repeat service and parts business, as well as referrals, for continuous growth.

But is advertising, the auto-mall concept or a great location the ultimate key to success for a dealership or retail business in today's competitive marketplace? The answer is an emphatic no!

THIS IS NOW . . .

Through my many years working with the number-one Japanese automobile maker, Toyota, and their luxury brand, Lexus, I've had the good fortune of visiting the number-one Toyota dealership in the United States, Longo Toyota, which has been owned by the Penske Group for over three decades. In my extensive travels across North America, I've also visited many other major, successful brands, both in and out of the auto-mall environment and, although location and marketing are key for any retail business, ultimate success comes down to leadership.

Leadership

Leadership that exemplifies an owner's or leader's psychology is the first key to business success. Owners and leaders who are most successful believe and practice the philosophy that customers must be treated right. And the only way to truly gain raving-fan customers who keep coming back is to first treat your staff right, with respect, courtesy and fairness.

> Leadership that exemplifies an owner's or leader's psychology is the first key to business success.

All too often, especially in the automotive retail world, I have seen owners who do not have respect for their staff. Unfortunately that attitude often results in high turnover rates, which leaves customers wondering and asking questions.

Truly satisfied customers who keep coming back and referring others do so because of positive personal experiences in dealing with staff, and are not loyal customers solely because of a businesses' product or location. It's the experience with the staff that matters most and that's why customers make referrals.

Staff members who deal directly with clients and who are treated well by management and owners consistently deliver the best service. This is simply because they're happier, and happy employees equal happy, loyal clients who keep coming back and referring others. That's how you maintain and build a loyal following.

The second most important fundamental for dealership success is undoubtedly innovation, and the third is marketing.

Innovation

Innovation is about creating exciting products, services and technologies, and continuously improving them to offer enhanced features and benefits to new and existing customers, and to meet new market trends and requirements.

As I mentioned in the introduction, I still actively sell at a major-market Lexus dealership, in a brand new facility that exemplifies innovation.

When clients drive into the climate-controlled service reception area, for example, they're greeted by an apprentice who drives their vehicle onto a highly sophisticated ground-level ramp area within the service reception area. A series of sensors are hooked up to the vehicle's wheels and engine compartment, which measure individual tire percentage wear, brake percentage wear, individual tire pressure, alignment and battery strength. The assessment includes a few other tests, with the results provided in a single-page report on the health of these critical areas of a client's vehicle. It may seem like a costly process, but it's a complimentary service for every client who visits, even those just in for an oil change.

In addition, the dealer principal added a second-tier executive lounge with card access, similar to those you find in airports. Designed mainly for clients who choose to wait for services to be completed (two hours or longer), the lounge provides guests with a more private working environment, enhanced comfort, and other conveniences, including roomy work areas, Wi-Fi, massage chairs and light meals.

This dealership is using technology and sophisticated machines, as well as innovative conveniences, to provide added value to clients, thus exceeding their expectations. Innovation can be developed through sales and service, as explained previously, and not just in new products and technology.

Innovation can be developed through sales and service or even continuously improving the way you work, and not just in new products and technology.

It's important to remember that innovation can be as simple as continuously improving the way you work, learning new sales techniques and best practices to become a more accomplished sales professional and provide your customers with a better purchase experience. This book is full of advice and suggestions for how you can be more innovative in your own sales role.

MARKETING STRATEGIES TO BUILD YOUR BUSINESS

The third fundamental, marketing, is finding creative and cost-effective ways to communicate the value of your product or service to existing and potential customers. And marketing works hand in hand with leadership and innovation. Without those two components, all the marketing in the world won't have much impact; it's essential that a healthy leadership mind-set and a culture of innovation are in place for all your marketing and sales efforts to bear maximum fruit.

In today's sophisticated and technology-filled world, marketing requires processes for creating and delivering value to customers, as well as customer relationship management, which benefits the entire organization as well as the individual sales professional.

Marketing is most effective when you take all of the following into consideration and develop strategies for each component: choose target markets, conduct market analysis and market segmentation, and understand customer behavior.

Identify Your Target Market

For any business, first understanding your ideal target market and demographic is key to how you source your business through marketing, advertising and community involvement. And for any retail sales associate or retail business, such as an auto dealership, to have long-term success, it's important to step out of the box in this modern, evolving time.

You must understand the demographic make-up of your marketplace, based on the types of businesses or industries surrounding your location, and whether it's a bedroom community, for example. This type of data is usually available on sites like Wikipedia, and all city or town websites will confirm income brackets, population, type of workforce and all vital statistics needed to understand your marketplace.

Some of the best and most commonly utilized information sources are available directly from the advertising agencies or outlets a retailer may use. For example, when our dealership advertises on various radio stations, in newspapers, or in other media, they are able to provide audited demographic data to assist in our decision-making on budgets, placements and so on. A radio station can tell you what age groups listen at what hours, what shows have higher listenership, and whether more listeners are driving or tuned into the radio outside of a car at any given time. A newspaper can tell you what their total readership is and suggest which sections are most popular; while digital media agencies can suggest ideal locations for digital media displays in public, outdoor locations, providing actual daily traffic counts and stats that gauge drive-by vehicle traffic or numbers of people walking by or through the location.

There are countless ways of marketing to your target audience, including the following:

- Use an existing database, such as all clients who have been active for the last two years (for example, in the car business you might aim a specific promotion at a particular segment of existing customers who are driving vehicles from the last four model years).

- Or, for targeting conquest business (new customers), you might choose to market to specific demographics, such as specific postal or zip codes based on income level, population, industry, etc.

Analyze and Segment Your Market

Market segmentation often works well in dealerships and involves dividing up the target market database into various segments, such as groups of customers who have previously purchased selected model years of specific cars or trucks. The group can then be targeted for upgrade events, private sales, service specials, new model introductions, VIP events, and for trade-ins of particular models to fill the pre-owned lots.

By continuously engaging existing clients through these types of events, customers are kept informed of a dealership's or business's current promotions, as well as new innovations in products or services. Most importantly, the marketing strategy continues to build valuable, long-lasting relationships through ongoing communications with existing customers.

You may also target new business with similar tactics. As discussed in the last section (Identify your Target Market), using demographics is the first and most common approach. Additional ways of targeting new business can include segmentation by geo-graphic area and psychographics, among others.

Geographic segmentation is targeting your new business by specific regions, for example identifying postal codes or a group of cities in your trading area to market to. For instance in Oakville, Ontario, we may target new business in other nearby cities such as West Mississauga, Burlington, Milton and Hamilton.

Market segmentation by psychographics is becoming increas-ingly popular as retailers seek new business based on consumers' interests and activities instead of demographics. Our dealership, for example, sets up car displays in an annual Humane Society Mutt Strutt event featuring dogs and their owners, as well as monthly Chamber of Commerce or local BIA events where potential new cli-ents are out browsing or participating at these community events.

Consumer Behavior

Before you can market and advertise to your target customers effectively, it is critical to understand not only who they are, but also what drives them to make a purchase.

> Buying decisions are affected by many different factors, including psychology, sociology, emotion, marketing and economics.

Take a typical client in our specific market area, we know the preferred method of acquiring a vehicle is first by leasing, then by cash and fewer by finance; however, in other markets customers may prefer financing over other methods, due to demographics like income level or job skill level, etc. With this knowledge of how our customers behave, we can focus our promotions and advertising accordingly.

Buying decisions are affected by many different factors, in-cluding psychology, sociology, emotion, marketing and economics to name a few. Today's tech-savvy consumers have easy access to a wealth of competitive products and service, so understanding what drives customers to select, secure, use or even dispose of products and services can help you be more strategic about your marketing efforts.

For example, some clients may choose to trade in their vehicles more often rather than keep an older vehicle with higher mileage and then have to sell it privately. These customers prefer the convenience and the status of always having a newer vehicle, and you can market to them differently.

Retail businesses that study and focus on their customers' needs and behavior will usually benefit the most from marketing and advertising, because they understand their clients and the marketplace much better.

METHODS OF MARKETING AND ADVERTISING

There are more ways of marketing available to you than ever before, and seemingly limitless avenues to advertise and promote your products and services. Some of the ways of reaching customers and prospects today should include, but are not limited to, the following.

Print Media

Despite significant changes in media consumption in recent years, it appears consumers still continue to trust in the power of the printed word when evaluating advertising. Dealerships usually can choose from a wide range of different types of newspapers and magazines, including local, regional, weekend editions, etc. Advertisers can purchase different sizes of space to display ads featuring editorial and photos; or full- and double-page spreads for promoting larger sales, deals or events. These types of ads can also feature high-quality color photos of inventory and facilities.

A perfect example of a print medium from the past is the *Auto-Trader* magazine, which has evolved from just a print magazine to a publication with a well-established online site (see below for more on online media), with thousands of cars available through phone apps, videos and links. For over twenty-five years, the *Auto-Trader* magazine dominated the used-car market, as the go-to magazine. It grew to include exclusive truck, bike, boat and even new vehicle magazines, due to the growth of the automotive industry with thousands of dealerships and strong readership.

Today, *Auto-Trader* is a strong online presence with its print format on the way out. However, print media remain very strong in specialized formats, such as weekly Wheels sections in various newspapers and magazines, which include editorial features on various topics, such as a dealership's community involvement or the industry news. Potential customers still like the idea of browsing through these special sections to see what grabs their attention. Readers usually trust what they see and read, which makes these specialized print options very viable for advertisers.

Billboard and Digital Signage

This is a major trend and increasingly popular, as billboards have evolved from huge, static paper ad displays to full digital and video content ads. These billboards are designed to display more vivid images and video content, to target consumers on the move.

These signs can now be found everywhere, including retail malls, airports, train stations, and strategic locations along major roads, highways and high-traffic areas. These are great media for advertising, as dealerships and retail businesses can more frequently change or update their ads to stay fresh, current and relevant, consistently capturing the attention of consumers who are on the move.

Call-to-Action Campaigns (Giveaways)

Whether you're attending trade shows, visiting the mall or even the supermarket, there are always opportunities to collect many free samples and other items given away by companies for promotional purposes.

A dealership, for example, might run a half-price tune-up special or a no-charge winter inspection just before the winter season. Although the dealership is giving something away for free or at very little charge, the value to the business is in the opportunity to up-sell and to build relationships with customers who do respond to these giveaways and promotional offers. You can usually determine the success of these campaigns by asking these simple questions:

- Are they really effective? You'll know quickly by the response rate.
- Do they get the message you're advancing across effectively?
- Is your message visible, clearly understood, and noticed enough?
- Is the giveaway unique, valuable, useful or just gimmicky?

You should consider these questions and more before implementing giveaways or call-to-action campaigns. In the retail dealership world, giveaway campaigns are nothing new and continue to be increasingly creative in an effort to drive more sales calls, appointments and walk-ins to the showroom. This can be a very simple but potentially effective marketing method. However, you must offer something useful and of some value, or don't bother.

Traditional Electronic Media (TV and Radio)

The television is virtually a member of our household, but with the advent of the Internet and social media, it is part of the older electronic media age. Whatever you're watching on TV, be it news, sports, movies or reality shows, advertising is everywhere. It's obvious that it's the most successful traditional electronic medium today, given the large audiences drawn and the millions charged for a sixty-second ad spot on sports events like the Super Bowl.

So many automobile dealer groups, larger dealerships and major retailers look to television for great exposure in their local and surrounding markets, effectively choosing airtime during key sports events, reality shows, weather and news programming to reach their target demographic. The electronic media business is down to a science of metrics, where TV and radio stations can tell you exactly who your audience is at all times of the day, and can recommend to dealerships and retailers the best times to target their audiences.

As a more affordable alternative to TV, radio is more commonly used by most established dealerships and retailers to target local markets. Most dealerships competing in our market area aim to be unique through the creativity of their radio ads. Some use celebrity voiceovers and endorsements to add credibility; and some even use kids' voices in an effort to captivate potential buyers.

Internet or Online (New Electronic Media)

It's not surprising that the newer electronic media are occupying more and more of our free time. The Internet is one of the most cost-effective and direct ways of creating awareness and of driving new business to a retail showroom today.

Entertainment sources, such as smart TVs, Internet, and social media sites like Facebook, are constantly chasing the consumer with many different types of incentives, surveys and promotions. New electronic media today offer more choices for advertising and promotion, such as online banners, mobile-phone marketing and personalized emails, where dealerships continue to capture a new, younger demographic through innovative marketing.

In many ways, marketing online has become the predominant and most economical way of communicating with customers and prospects, and can be just as effective (if not more so) than traditional advertising; therefore, dealerships and retailers should use some of the following ways to source and grow their business through online marketing and advertising.

- **Press Releases:** One of the fastest ways to spread news about your dealership or retail store is by sending out an email press release to your database or a list of email prospects. Today there are many online software packages and services that simply need only the email addresses and a message, and they can get the word out and track all the metrics pertaining to open rates and click-through rates, etc.

  Be sure to refer to your local anti-spam legislation before conducting an email blast of any kind. At our dealership, we've announced grand openings, our move to a new location, new model introductions and launches, charity and community events, while attracting new and repeat business at the same time.

- **Share knowledge:** Since major retailers should be experts in their field, it's a great marketing tool and practice to share expert knowledge with your customer base. This can include service tips and advice, winter driving recommendations, spring gardening tips and even recipes.

  Combining valuable information with irresistible offers and call-to-action campaigns (as discussed above) will help a retailer to capture a potential client's information. This allows you to create a relationship going forward and is one critical step in lead generation. Sharing of expert knowledge comes down to offering ongoing valuable information in return for building relationships.

- **Create a newsletter:** Online newsletters, when done well, are an increasingly effective way of staying in contact with your clients. It costs a lot to gain customers and they're very easy to lose, so why not try to stay better connected with them through an e-newsletter? I was directly involved in initiating, creating and launching the first e-newsletter for our dealership and was shocked by the high open and click rates—almost three times the industry average.

  When links and tags are included in e-newsletters, you can measure every click to discover what content caught your customer's attention, gaining valuable feedback on their interests. A newsletter can include service and sales specials and incentives, new-product release news, videos, articles, coupons, announcements, and lots more.

- **Video marketing:** In today's marketing and advertising world, most dealerships and retailers look for effective and unique ways to stand out, often while competing for the same potential client. In an effort to invest their marketing dollars more wisely, many dealerships have begun creating their own online commercials and catchy information videos, including new product presentation videos, and basic how-to service demos, such as changing a flat tire, programming phones, using GPS systems, programming and operating garage openers, etc.

  The dealership I work at created its own personal music video including most of the staff dancing and singing to a popular song while showing off our new facility. This music video produced by a dealership turned out to be the first of its kind and received worldwide reviews while conveying a get-to-know-us, welcoming atmosphere.

Although many were skeptical to begin with, the video turned out to be one of the most successful marketing moves in the entire history of our dealership, gathering tens of thousands of online views from potential clients and competitors alike. It was a great way to attract new business, using just one successful, unique and exclusive video to show off the new, innovative facility.

Social Media

As you can see, marketing and advertising today are fundamentally different than they were before, and you will soon understand why the days of simply waiting for clients to show up to your showroom will lead you to very little success. Today's clients come to you from many different avenues; some of them you will never even see until it's time for them to take delivery of your product or service because much of the sales process takes place in the virtual world. For example, just in the past week I put together seven deals from several sources. Three were lease renewals, three were new clients to the dealership, and one was a referral. Three of the seven deals were completed via phone and emails, while the rest visited the dealership only once or twice. The one thing they all had in common is that they all did some product research online and had already been connected with the dealership via social media outreach or some sort of promotions in the past.

Using social media strategically in your marketing efforts is now critical to your future and success in the new age of automotive and retail selling. You may be doing some of this already, but you may not be capturing the full potential of social media if you haven't planned properly and strategically.

Once you've decided to engage your potential audience with social media, it's about maximizing every potential opportunity to spread the word about your products and services.

- **First utilize at least three credible major social media programs.** The first order of business should be to contact all your friends and acquaintances on Facebook, LinkedIn and other social media sites. Build up your social media presence as a tool to share new product information, incentives, special events, and milestones, like company anniversaries, private sales, etc. And with every vehicle sold you can ask your new clients to like your page and spread the word to their friends.

- **Use LinkedIn pages to work for you while you're sleeping** by updating your career path and accomplishments as well as notable career promotions, milestones and events. All smart investors make money in their sleep and the retail business is no different today, with technology that can work for you. You can offer creative incentives for people to like your page and spread the word to build your own customer base. For example, you can encourage your contacts to sign up for future offers or give them the opportunity to enter a draw to win a prize. Remember, every positive sales and service experience, and every instance of good customer feedback, is a perfect time to ask for referrals and for your clients to like your Facebook page, post a positive review and connect through other social media.

Direct Mail and Email Campaigns

Direct mail and email campaigns can be very effective ways to reach out to existing and prospective clients, and these campaigns can usually be quite easily managed. They can be in the form of creative letters, postcards or email blasts, for example, and can be used effectively to promote products, upgrades to existing clients, seasonal offerings, specials, or service promotions

to parts and service clients. This is a simple way to continue engaging and building relationships with your client base, as well
as to target and communicate with new potential customers, as
long as you take the following into consideration when designing
your campaign.

- **You must identify who the target is for your direct
  mail piece or email.** You can usually use search criteria
  and parameters in your database to choose the specific
  customers you want to extend a particular offer to. For
  instance, 2010 to 2012 model years of a particular vehicle,
  whether sold or leased; or any active clients in a particular
  time frame, such as the last three years.

- **Your direct mail or email campaign must have a
  timeline and expiry** to create urgency for your prospects
  or customers to respond, therefore providing more accurate, measurable results and feedback.

- **Include key offer(s) or tactics.** Is the offer clearly defined
  and useful enough for the clients to respond? Will the
  offer improve or enhance the customer's situation, and
  provide clear benefits to the client? Does your offer match
  the needs of the potential customer? Those questions must
  be answered in your offer, or your letter will be a waste
  of time and postage. The bottom line here is selling the
  benefits, not the features.

- **Your direct mail or email campaign must have a
  follow-up sequence.** Too many companies choose and
  attempt direct mail or email as a marketing strategy and
  don't follow up for various reasons, including lack of success or response. You must have a strategy for sequential

mailings monthly or quarterly in order to excel over your competition. Clients will often not respond to your first outreach, so it's important to communicate your offer several times over a predetermined time period. I have clients tell me every time I do my quarterly mailings that they've received my previous letters or emails, but the second or third is the one that finally got them to react. Direct mail and email are forms of personalized advertising that, with enough repetition, can drive clients in the door. So, use direct mail and emails with some frequency, not just once, to generate leads rather than sales. Once you get the leads, respond in person, phone or email, and then target the sale.

- **Headlines make all the difference in direct marketing.** Clients are swamped today with all sorts of advertisements from electronic, print, digital and online marketing, so your headline must stand out and be relevant to your target customer. Most clients don't pay attention to advertising, so to get them into your showroom, other than when they want to visit, you must have an attention-grabbing headline that shakes them to move and contact you. Write down multiple choices of headlines before choosing one. If you can't get their attention with the headline, then the rest of the letter won't matter.

- **Personalize your communication.** To increase the response rates of your direct mail and email campaigns dramatically, your message must be personalized and include a unique value-added proposition. From the selected headline to the main message and enclosed offer, everything must stand out in a unique way to differentiate you from the other marketing pieces.

Even the envelope enclosing your letter must be good or your potential lead won't make it to the letter. The best way to get past the envelope is to handwrite the addresses, which makes it very personal. If that's not possible due to volume, then make specific references by name, make and model of car, lease or loan expiry date, time remaining on their lease or loan etc. For existing clients, the letters I've created and used successfully over the last three years all have a personal account of each client's affairs so the letter speaks directly to them and addresses their specifics, therefore capturing their attention.

Private Sales Campaigns

A unique way of tapping into your existing customer database and obtaining much higher closing ratios is to host private sales. Bringing existing clients together for a private, invitation-only event not only helps to boost sales, but also is an extremely effective way to build a stronger relationship with existing customers. Private sales with proper timing, planning and implementation can almost guarantee up to double your normal closing ratio and deals. Private sales have evolved over the years to be more manageable, predictable and profitable for dealers and retail outlets alike.

These events usually create a great atmosphere at the dealership, with showrooms, lots and displays all arranged to generate additional excitement. Private sales are usually fully staffed for better attention to customers and are often catered, with complimentary refreshments and food to make the clients feel more valued and at ease. Always find ways to slow your customers down; providing food and attention always encourages them to linger and engage with you or your staff and, therefore, works to maximize your sales opportunities.

To ensure the effectiveness and success of your next private sale, develop a key strategy with the following guidelines:

- **Pick a weekday, preferably Wednesday or Thursday.** The date is important and can have a huge impact on your overall success. Weekdays are better because business hours are usually longer than on weekends, giving more clients more timing options to take advantage of your promotions. Another advantage of a mid-week date is flexibility. If a private sale is on a Wednesday or Thursday, it makes for better preparation beforehand, with at least two business days to get ready at the beginning of the week, and better follow-up time afterwards, allowing you time to maximize on potential leads before the weekend.

- **Select a target list.** Your invitation list is crucial to your private-sale success and must be managed and targeted well. As mentioned earlier, before you start choosing lists of names, make sure you know what you currently have, who you're targeting and why. If you have a larger portfolio of 5,000 or more existing clients, you should segment the list into two, based on the size of your sales staff working the event. Market segmentation can be decided by model year or age of vehicle if you're targeting certain higher-end models, or by postal or zip codes to target a certain demographic. It's also a good idea to segment by date, checking when that particular segment was targeted last, so you don't overwhelm them with invitations. You want to avoid being ignored, or inadvertently making the sale or event less interesting and effective.

- **Choose an event theme or headline.** As with direct mail, the headline of your event is a priority. What will you title the event? Is it an annual, semi-annual or year-end event? Will it be titled an "Exclusive Upgrade Event," or will you choose a theme based on current trends?

Recently we had two new model launches and a major model redesign. These make great themes or headlines, such as "Important Details about the 4th Generation RX," or "Introducing the All-New 2016 Lexus RX," or, "You Are Invited to our Club Lexus Event," or "You Are Invited to Preview the New 2015 NX."

- **Send out designed letters or e-blasts to your target list.** Have a creative marketing piece designed specifically for the event; ensure that it fits the occasion and that it has an impactful, noticeable headline. If it's an e-blast, make sure the invitation is embedded into the email and pops the minute it's opened. Then express a colorful, bold message announcing your event, making each client feel exclusive and special with personalization, crisp images and a short, direct, point-by-point list clearly stating your offers and benefits.

  You should make certain you provide the option to RSVP and encourage appointments, both of which help to create urgency and immediate responses. The initial letter or e-blast serves to generate immediate responses through appointments and also serves as the first introduction, which justifies a follow-up phone call. Your message must include a timeline or deadline to create urgency, appointments and confidence in the event.

- **Follow-up phone calls.** To get the most out of a private sale event, you can hire an agency that specializes in private sales events, or dedicate at least two in-house, skilled telephone people to schedule and confirm appointments for maximum organization and results. After you've chosen your target list and completed your mailing and/or e-blast, this list is handed over to the agency or to staff to make the follow-up phone calls to the majority who didn't RSVP. Investing the time and/or money to make follow-up calls in advance of the event itself usually increases the number of appointments significantly, because they serve as a follow-up to the marketing invitation you already sent, giving an effective conversation point for the call. Remember, as we touched on in chapter 3, Best Practices of Top Sales Performers, if you don't have a reason to call, it's an uphill battle from the get-go and probably a waste of time. The most effective sales calls are planned and strategized with clear objectives and benefits to offer the potential client.

Now that your list of appointments is ready, your sales team is poised, and the stage is set with a decorated showroom, finger foods and drinks, the agency (if you've hired one) would usually supply at least two greeters to properly register and monitor your customers as they arrive. If you haven't hired an agency to help organize and manage the event, make sure you have in-house staff assigned to, and ready to perform, this task.

The greeters or associates dedicated to managing the event not only manage the traffic flow, they are also great at prequalifying and segmenting those who show up for the sale. Using a short questionnaire, your greeters can easily identify which attendees are more or less ready to buy and can direct the most qualified leads to the appropriate sales staff.

I've been involved in numerous private sales over the years, and with proper organization you can usually account for every walk-in, every gift or incentive you handed out, and ultimately every vehicle sold. With all that information at hand, you should be able to determine an accurate closing ratio and to summarize your efforts and, ultimately, the success of the event.

Networking

We've talked about the importance of networking earlier in
the book, for advancing your own career and improving your
effectiveness as a sales professional. In addition to helping you
continuously improve in your role personally, networking can be
an effective marketing strategy as well—a key way to grow your
business over the long term, individually and as an organization.
Following are some suggestions for how you can turn networking
moments into marketing opportunities.

- **Use every avenue available for individual networking:**
  You just never know where the next client or the next
  great marketing opportunity will come from, so seek out
  new contacts and ideas every chance you get. Start with
  friends, relatives, community groups and organizations,
  churches, legions, service clubs, sports teams—expand
  your social circles and personal contacts, and don't be
  shy about explaining what you do or about asking them
  tactfully for referrals.

  You should source networking opportunities through
  clients, friends and organized groups such as BNI, or
  other business networking groups that bring selected
  members of other local businesses together as a source of
  direct referrals.

- **Offer incentives for referrals:** Put a formal program in
  place, offering each client you meet or sell to a reason or
  incentive to refer more business to you. For example, you
  could offer a referral fee to your existing clients for each
  new contact they connect you with. Your clients have
  their own personal and professional networks, and they
  can be a rich source of prospective business. Marketing to

the networks of your networks can be a very effective way of broadening your base of clients and prospects.

- **Tap into your own service department:** Each day, as many as forty or fifty or more customers will walk into a large dealership for service and parts, and many will wander into the showroom to browse or wait around in comfortable lounges. It's important to keep an eye out for these clients, especially early in the morning when customers drop off their cars for service and are waiting for a ride or a shuttle.

  Many parts and service clients who walk into your showroom will engage in conversation and represent prospects for immediate or future business themselves, or an opportunity for additional referrals. Remember, if they're coming to your dealership for service, they are already your existing client even if they didn't originally purchase their vehicle from your dealership. You can meet these guests directly, obtain contact information and become a trusted contact. These clients are also in your company database and are a perfect target for direct marketing campaigns.

  Many service clients wander into the showroom only to have a new model or color pique their interest and most times there's no one to speak to. Choose at least two mornings per week to be in early in order to be prepared for, and take to advantage of, these potential clients who are right under your nose. Remember action gets results!

- **Community networking:** Community networking and marketing are becoming increasingly effective in gaining great exposure and direct leads while building valuable

community relations. Many dealerships and retailers
today take their products and services out into the community to connect with potential customers.

These types of events can include, for example,
displays in shopping malls or mall parking lots; these
busy public venues draw a wide range of shoppers from
all demographics and offer potential clients the chance to
browse at their own pace without the fear of being ap-
proached by a sales representative, and then to contact or
visit a retailer later.

Other creative, popular and effective venues for
getting out into the community with your product are entertainment venues like sports arenas, stadiums or concert
halls, and even in busy airports. In short, places or venues
with high consumer traffic or crowds represent great
exposure and marketing opportunities to big numbers of
potential clients.

- **Charity events:** Consider cooperating with a charitable
  organization to benefit both parties and do some good in
  the community while you build your business. For example, your dealership could donate a vehicle for a charity
  auction or prize draw. The charitable organization pro-
  motes the event heavily, solicits bids for the vehicle or
  sells tickets for it, and raises funds in the process. What's
  in it for you? These fundraisers usually come with spon-
  sorship programs, where the retailer or business donating
  the prize receives great exposure through printed mate-
  rials, direct marketing campaigns, exclusive live sponsor
  mentions, product displays, digital and other promotional
  signage, ballroom table displays and/or invaluable networking opportunities such as direct interaction with a
  room full of potential clients.

As you can see, there is an enormous range of marketing methods available to you. Although you may not use them all, you need to be aware of the various marketing strategies you can take advantage of and how to use them effectively to build your business. It's also important not to pick just one marketing medium and stick with it, even if it is effective for you. You need to consider the appropriate marketing mix—the best combination of strategies to create awareness and increase sales for your business. For example, an effective print advertising campaign combined with a direct mail campaign to specific customers can be far more effective in generating leads and closing sales than either one of those marketing methods used on its own. To decide on the ideal marketing mix for you or your company, you need to start by establishing your marketing goals.

YOUR MARKETING GOALS

To be an effective marketer, you must be clear about your goals. Will your campaign be aimed at existing customers or new client base? A combination of both? Campaigns can be designed to communicate and motivate, promote and increase brand recognition; you need to establish up front the purpose and goal of your campaign before jumping in to decide which marketing medium or strategy to use.

For example, brand recognition is essential, especially in the retail automobile industry where numerous competitors are vying for the same customers. But which of the marketing methods above would be most appropriate to use to boost brand recognition? Community networking or a direct mail campaign would likely do more in this instance to accomplish your marketing goal than would a private sale (for existing customers already familiar with your brand) or a giveaway campaign.

And if you do choose to hand out promotional items as part of another of your marketing efforts, what will you choose as a giveaway item, and how will you give it away? This one key point can determine your campaign's success or failure. In my many years of retail automotive and advertising, I've observed, participated in and created many marketing and advertising campaigns. One of the key elements to success or failure is offering a giveaway that is useful and measurable.

For example, useful could mean offering a discount coupon for winter tire packages at the start of the season, when it's actually relevant and needed by consumers. Not only does a promotional offer like that add value for the customer, it also creates additional service department write-ups or work orders, yielding additional direct customer pay (CP) hours from the initial coupon offer. (Dealerships and retailers always aim to generate more revenue as a result of work done for and paid for by the customer [CP hours], as opposed to work that comes from warranty claims or internal work orders.)

And in any marketing campaign it's important to measure your success: Keep track of the number of inquires, sales and giveaways relative to the amount of potential buyers you targeted.

Always start with the purpose for your marketing efforts so you can be effective in choosing the right marketing mix to use to accomplish your goals, and in measuring the success of your campaign when it's all said and done.

MANAGING YOUR MARKETING RESOURCES

In closing this chapter, here are some sample questions that will give you a more in-depth understanding of your market so you can better budget marketing dollars, and have a focused approach to advertising as a salesperson or manager. One key piece of data that you will gather from your market analysis is where advertising and marketing efforts as well as budgets should be focused.

As a salesperson, sales manager or owner, this information can mean the difference between success and failure—for you as an individual and for the business in general—so it's important to continuously and accurately research and analyze your market.

Sample Market Analysis Questions:

- What type of workforce makes up your market area?
- Is there a historic high or low approval rate on loans and leases for your store?
- Do your clients trade or upgrade vehicles often, say every two to three years?
- How many vehicles and drivers are in the average household?
- Do most or a greater number of clients commute using public transportation due to traffic congestion or proximity to work?
- On weekends does a lot of your market area travel out of town to vacation spots such as cottages, or do you get a lot of weekend shoppers?
- Do you get steady traffic after work hours?
- How much of your traffic is from outside of your market area and why do they come to your dealership or retail establishment's location?
- Is your location a destination location, where clients literally have to make a conscious decision to attend your location?
- Is your location in a high-traffic, high-exposure area that attracts business from many other markets?
- What type of media do your target customers absorb? Newspapers, magazine, radio, television, digital signage, email blasts or e-newsletter, or primarily social media?

We've covered a lot of ground in this chapter, and that's because effective marketing is key to your success in sales. You can improve your sales techniques and better yourself as a sales professional, but if you don't attract the prospects, customers and referrals, you won't have anyone to sell to. Effective marketing is at the core of growing your business and, therefore, is an essential ingredient in your sales success.

In the chapters that follow, we'll return to sales fundamentals, revealing many more techniques you can apply to improve and grow in your role.

SUMMARY

- **Leadership style matters.** Leadership based on the owner's or leader's psychology is the first key to success. Those who are the most successful believe and practice the philosophy that customers must be treated right, and that the only way to truly gain raving-fan customers who keep coming back is to first treat your staff right, with respect, courtesy and fairness.

- **Customer Relationships.** Clients who keep coming back and referring others are motivated by their personal experiences and relationships with your staff, not just by product, facility or location. It's the positive experience with the person they're dealing with that matters most, that prompts them to make referrals and that builds valuable, long-term customer relationships.

- **Customer Service.** Staff members who deal directly with clients and are treated well by management and owners ultimately deliver the best service—consistently. They are simply happier, and happy employees equal happy, loyal clients who keep coming back.

- **Long-term dealership and retailer success requires both innovation and marketing** to meet the evolving needs of your market, and to reach and communicate with your existing and potential customers effectively.

- **Innovation** is about continuous improvement, creating new and exciting products, services and technologies that offer enhanced features and benefits to new and existing customers to meet their evolving needs.

- **Marketing** is finding creative, cost-effective ways of communicating the value of your product or service to your existing and potential customers.

- **Identify Your Target Market:** For any business, first understanding your ideal customers and demographic is key to how you grow your business through marketing, advertising and community involvement.

- **Market Segmentation** often works well in dealerships and retail establishments and involves dividing up the target market database into segments or groups, such as selected model years of specific cars or trucks, or by product design or price ranges.

- **Consumer Behavior:** Before you can market and advertise to your target customers effectively, it is critical to understand not only who they are, but also what drives them to make a purchase. Buying decisions are affected by many different factors, including psychology, sociology, emotion, marketing and economics.

- **Some of the most effective methods of marketing today should include, but are not limited to, the following;**
  - Print media
  - Billboard and digital signage

- Call-to-Action campaigns (giveaways)
- Traditional electronic media (TV and radio)
- Internet or Online (New electronic media)
- Social media
- Direct mail and email campaigns
- Private sales campaigns
- Networking

- **Marketing Goals:** To be an effective marketer, you must be clear about your goals; you need to establish up front the purpose and goal of your campaign before jumping in to decide which marketing medium or strategy to use.

- **Marketing Resources:** You should be constantly researching and analyzing your market in order to determine where advertising and marketing efforts as well as budgets should be focused.

CHAPTER 6

CREATING A POSITIVE PURCHASE AND SERVICE EXPERIENCE

After a total of twenty-five years in automotive sales, marketing and advertising, I've summarized many reasons why clients bought from me, and from the dealerships and advertising organizations that I've represented. To date, I've had direct involvement in over 6,200 auto deals and over 10,000 advertising and marketing contracts over the years; this experience has allowed me to gather some key facts, case studies and successes that I can share with you to help you improve on your own relationships with your clients.

Some of the direct feedback I received from clients over the years, and their reasons for buying, were obvious and simple. Customers were tired of looking around, they hated the process of shopping for a car or buying advertising, or maybe they finally met someone who connected with them and made the buying process a more positive experience. While service and pricing are at the top of the list for most car buyers, the one thing that motivates shoppers to choose one dealer or retailer over another is a positive purchasing or dealer experience.

Retail sales (and the automotive industry specifically) have struggled for decades to deliver customer service at a high level, so much so that customers have, in fact, even lowered their expectations of the service they'll receive in these industries. In my decades of experience, I've always viewed this as an opportunity to sell more and make more money.

The deficiencies of other individuals or companies present you with key opportunities, not just to be better than they are, but also to differentiate yourself from the pack in general. How you choose to approach dealing with your customers and prospects can make your clients' purchase experience not just a positive one, but something really special and different in the world of customer service they encounter. You can even make them feel like they are more of a "guest in your home" and exceed their expectations of the service experience.

This may come as a surprise to some, but truly successful sales reps and organizations today have one thing in common: They're good at relationship building, and at delivering and maintaining a great purchasing and/or service experience.

Clients today are looking for convenience, value, professional advice and consultation; they want prompt friendly service, solutions, and a go-to person or organization they can rely on to deliver on their current and future needs. Clients today are frankly way too busy and will not accept sub-standard service; most are even willing to pay a little more for added perceived value. This is why some clients will drive past other, similar brands for an hour or more to seek out service where they're more comfortable, have established relationships and get a more pleasant overall service experience.

Creating and nurturing raving-fan clients will help you establish and grow your customer base; in fact, turning good customers into your biggest fans is at the foundation of a successful sales career or business. Over the last twenty-five years, I've learned many lessons from clients about providing excellent service; this chapter covers some of the fundamentals of building your customer relationship skills and creating a path for sales success.

VALUE

The first step in creating an excellent service experience for your customers is defining and delivering value. If you learn how to master the value proposition, you're well on your way. It's one of the biggest factors in a client's decision today, bringing the whole purchase experience together and leading them to purchase from you.

- **The bottom line is to add more value than anyone else and you will win more clients.** Value is often misconstrued as offering the lowest price or the biggest discount, but that's far from true in today's marketplace of tech-savvy and busy consumers. You can add and offer value in many ways that are not directly connected to pricing, and still affect a buyer's decision. There's value even in making your clients feel appreciated just for making the call or visiting your showroom.

- **First listen to your clients' key needs and desires and only then present an overall value proposition.** Value is perceived, so why would you think you know what means more to a client, only focusing on price or payments, for example? Price and payments should be the last thing you discuss after you've determined the client's needs and established value based on what's important to them.

Break down any important added incentives or perks that your dealership or establishment offers and defer discussing price until after you've outlined your list of valuable features and benefits. For example, your establishment may offer value-added perks, such as valet and shuttle service, free car washes or basic detailing when clients have their vehicle in for service, free Wi-Fi, comfortable executive lounges and refreshments, service and sales coupons, and various seasonal promotions. Other loyalty incentives could include lifetime battery changes for remote keys, free annual outings like golf tournaments, or invitations to charity and community events.

When the value picture is laid out clearly first, you have a foundation for a quicker and more informed commitment. You also raise the bar for the competition to overcome, and you can command more money for your products and services.

CONVENIENCE

Convenience today is a very big deal for consumers, given their busy lifestyles and a vast range of demographics. You can offer your clients convenience in various ways. For example, you can make booking service appointments much easier for them by offering technology solutions so they can schedule appointments online. You can also offer extended service hours, courtesy cars, valet or shuttle service and much more. Many dealerships have also undergone major renovations or built innovative, ultra-modern facilities aimed at attracting new clients and providing higher levels of comfort and convenience for existing clients as well as staff.

Emphasizing the conveniences you offer to the customer makes negotiating a deal much easier for you and your prospective client, as you've already established a substantial value proposition before even beginning to talk about the deal itself.

Most modern dealerships and retailers now have dedicated business development departments that coordinate service appointments and other time-saving benefits for clients. Others have implemented Internet departments dedicated to handling online sales leads, live chats, e-marketing, advertising and social media, all of which make it much easier for your customers to communicate with you—and easier for them to do business with you.

On the sales side, some dealerships offer indoor pre-owned showrooms and delivery bays for added convenience. The sales departments can usually offer other money-making conveniences, such as on-the-spot financing options, rust proofing, accessories and protection features like warranties and insurance. Offering these kinds of benefits creates one-stop shopping convenience for customers and provides them with a great deal of added value.

The bottom line is, show off the conveniences of your facility to inform the potential buyer what's available to them and build more value. This makes negotiating a deal much easier for you and your prospective client, as you've already established a substantial value proposition before even beginning to talk about the deal itself.

SERVICE

What defines a great dealership or retailer is successfully delivering over-the-top customer service. Although a dealership or a retailer may expand, build new facilities, and commit resources to training its staff or improving internal processes to make the service and buying experience more efficient, without a solid base of repeat and referral business, the potential for growth and real success is limited.

Creating an excellent service experience for your customers is only possible if the staff are highly motivated, enjoy their work environment, are eager to embrace new challenges and changes and, of course, are fairly incentivized and compensated. I've seen many instances where service is over-emphasized in theory, but nothing close to good service actually gets delivered. I've witnessed numerous times where more challenging customer concerns and issues are avoided or deflected to other departments, eventually leading to a poor service experience.

Happier employees are the ones more inclined to exceed customer expectations and play a paramount role in delivering an enhanced purchase and service experience.

Retailers wonder why it's a constant struggle with disgruntled customers and staff, and why no one steps up to the task of listening and being accountable to providing a solution. Happier employees are the ones more inclined to exceed customer expectations and play a paramount role in delivering an enhanced purchase and service experience. Customers are more likely to love a company if the employees first do and, therefore, convey enthusiasm and a positive attitude to the clients they're dealing with.

ACCOUNTABILITY

Any sales and service team needs to be accountable in order to deliver the best overall customer experience. Sales is the lifeblood of any business, whether from your main product line (such as new or used vehicles, or business office products), or after-sales parts and service.

I've worked at dealerships where a greater emphasis was placed on other supporting departments, such as administration, rather than on the sales function. In other words, management and ownership constantly expected sales to deliver more and held them more accountable than other departments, but certainly showed them less appreciation. Unfortunately, the end result is that auto sales reps are treated as lower-class positions by co-workers in other departments, and even by customers who may themselves hold sales positions in other fields.

Naturally, any sales team who grinds out deals and constantly drives revenue will be held accountable daily by employers, and by the customers they encounter. But they should also be acknowledged, respected, and rewarded appropriately; only then will they be encouraged to be more accountable and to provide an enhanced purchase experience to every customer daily.

It is in the best interest of ownership and management to have a motivated sales team that is onside and committed to the overall success of the company. When they are valued, respected and treated fairly, they are willing to be held to higher levels of accountability. This is really only possible when mutual respect exists between management and staff, and when all are philosophically focused on the same goal: to deliver a consistent level of higher service.

Here are six steps for management and sales teams, on how they can hold one another accountable to deliver a more impactful customer experience:

- **Management and sales should discuss why accountability is important,** and should support each other to accomplish individual and company goals. This certainly doesn't mean micro-management; rather, it's about informing a sales and service team about the fundamental culture and policies of the company and highlighting the importance of everyone's individual role to the overall success.

- **Establish clearly defined goals and metrics.** With sales it's all about the numbers. Surprisingly, most of the sales colleagues that I've worked with have never really set and monitored individual sales targets, let alone concerned

themselves with team metrics or overall dealership targets. "We'll sell as much as we can," or, "I'll give it my
best shot," are common refrains but are neither specific
targets nor measurable goals. This type of vague approach
leads to mediocre performance at best, a lack of accountability and underachievement in general, all of which in
turn leads to even lower levels of accountability and sub-
standard results—a vicious cycle of under-performance.

Management and sales teams must clearly define
annual and monthly targets and use metrics to track
progress on goals, such as pending and completed sales,
numbers of clients engaged, sales calls and e-leads
received; and on the service side, numbers such as the
amount of customer pay hours booked and sold. Too
many variables will complicate the process, so don't
try to measure everything; but all sales staff should be
held accountable to basic metrics and be able to answer
questions relating to their individual performance. If
expectations for customer service are outlined and appropriate measures clearly set, accountability for delivering a
better service experience can then be tracked and quanti-
fied more easily.

- **Break down overall dealership goals into individual
targets and keep the sales and service teams accountable.** (See also chapter 4, the Action Plan, for more detail
on this topic.) In 1999-2000, I managed a sales team at a
Toyota store to a record 937 deliveries, which represented a thirty-seven percent increase over the prior year, a
record which was still standing in 2014. At that time, we
were just beginning to use computers for basic reports and
I remember expanding on a basic Excel spreadsheet the
owner had designed for monthly sales tracking.

The goal I set for the sales team of eight was 1,000 units for calendar year 1999, a forty-seven percent increase year over year. I had a vision and a belief that this could be done even though many were skeptical. But at the end of the day I had buy-in from the sales team to give it a shot. So, I broke down the 1,000 units based on each individual salesperson's strengths (that is, assigning higher individual targets to stronger sales reps or those with more experience, rather than simply dividing the total target evenly across all sales reps); then I also broke it down by month, by model, and some other basic criteria. I then presented my plan to the team and monitored progress closely to the end of the year; we actually got close, delivering 937 vehicles.

Today, that spreadsheet has evolved to a more sophisticated tool, including income goals, percentage variances, percentage of total target reached and many other metrics. The key to sales accountability is to simplify big, overall goals into smaller bite-sized targets that clarify the goals for each individual and for smaller time periods, and then implement an action plan to achieve them.

- **Create a competitive team sales board or individual log to track progress on the metrics being measured.** The sales team should record their numbers daily and report them at least weekly during an overall review in a team sales meeting. They should also be prepared to be challenged. This weekly visibility amongst the team creates constructive competition and should help to motivate those who are lagging to catch up or take the lead. Accountability to one's self is as important as accountability to the team's success, so no one should be let off the hook if they haven't delivered. Constructive individual and team feedback helps to keep everyone accountable and on track for the greater goal of selling more and delivering the ultimate purchase and service experience for the customer.

My Personal Spreadsheet of Metrics

Here is a partial snapshot of the spreadsheet I've been using for over three years, summarizing monthly and annual sales targets for two brands as well as some partial income numbers. This graphic is similar to the version we saw back in chapter 3; like that one, the table on the facing page is only an excerpt from a much larger, more complicated spreadsheet that I use to track a number of different metrics. Although the table to the right doesn't show all the information I capture (because space is limited here), it serves to illustrate the point that you should always be tracking your actual progress against your targets.

With this spreadsheet as my guide, I always know where I stand and I don't need anyone else to suggest what targets I should be doing. In this example, my personal target shows 220 and actual deliveries show 191 (well beyond anyone else's actual sales in the two stores I represented). Although I did sell over 200 vehicles, a few did not actually get delivered in the 2013 sales year due to lack of financing or availability, etc.

To enhance accountability and overall productivity, implement the following practices in your sales team:

- **Acknowledge and celebrate accomplishments.** In most automotive and retail sales environments, not enough emphasis is placed on acknowledging sales accomplishments. Accountability and individual drive can dwindle rapidly if a sales team or individual is not acknowledged for achieving targets, making a dedicated effort, or for delivering a consistently great purchase and service experience.

TOYOTA #'S					LEXUS #'S		
MONTH	2013 # DLVD	SALES 2013			MONTH	# DLVD	2013
JAN	15	15			JAN	1	1
FEB	14	14			FEB	0	0
MAR	15	15			MAR	1	1
APR	8	9			APR	3	3
MAY	16	17			MAY	9	9
JUNE	12	12	**170** new target		JUNE	4	4
JULY	16	16	**14 TOY FR GOAL**		JULY	3	3
AUG	16	16			AUG	1	1
SEPT	8	9			SEPT	2	2
OCT	16	16			OCT	4	4
NOV	13	14			NOV	5	6
DEC	7	8			DEC	2	1
		161					35
	156	Target	plus/mns			35	Target
AVG	13.00	14.17	-1.17		AVG	2.92	4.167
			target	YTD	% of Target	FR GL	
		Toy target	170	156	91.76%	14	
		Lexus target	50	35	70.00%	15	
		Totals	220	191	86.82%		
		avg/ mth	18.33	17.36	94.71%		
					$ 5,060.67	com	
		ECP% SOLD	47.00%		$ 253.03	bonus	5%
	SLS AWAY	DEL'S AWAY		TOYOTA	$ 1,000.00	bonus	gross
					$ 600.00	bonus	csi
	-4	-9			$ 1,000.00	Lexus	Lexus
					$ 1,730.00	Other	
					$ 9,643.70	total	

Sales managers should identify, acknowledge, celebrate and reward all such achievements to build high energy and momentum for sales teams or individuals. Individual acknowledgment can mean a lot, even for the smallest deeds. For example, you can publicly recognize an employee by sharing an example of where and how they exceeded customer expectations by delivering over the top service; or you could simply thank a sales rep publicly or privately for a major contribution towards overall team targets.

Other good ways to celebrate accomplishments are via an employee of the month award, an acknowledgment for mentoring peers, or even a simple thank-you for handling a customer complaint or issue. Sometimes it's the small, simple things that managers do to recognize employees that mean the most, and they can even go much further to making that person feel valued and appreciated than any monetary rewards or compensation ever could.

- **Weekly debriefs and feedback during sales meetings build on accountability and responsibility.** At the Lexus dealership where I currently work, we dedicate a few minutes at each meeting, sometimes twice weekly, to listen to feedback from each other. This safe, open environment encourages us all to share some of the best ideas, experiences and opportunities with one another, helping us all to improve and succeed.

  It's critical to ensure that feedback in these meetings is both honest and respectful, to make sure that all salespeople feel comfortable. It's also a great time to turn all the factors that otherwise may de-motivate a sales team into opportunities for growth and success, by allowing for constructive criticism and feedback. We discuss customer

feedback, actual deal scenarios, objections, product updates, service, compensation and any general thoughts
aimed at improving overall efficiency through responsibility and accountability.

EMPOWERMENT

This can be the most powerful and effective tool available to an
employee in any business. Empowerment means having the resources, motivation, skills and authority to be responsible and
accountable for the outcomes of one's own actions while addressing customer issues.

Empowerment means having the resources, motivation, skills
and authority to be responsible and accountable
for the outcomes of one's own actions while
addressing customer issues.

For eight years, I travelled extensively across North America
and parts of the Caribbean, witnessing some of the best examples of accountability first-hand through my dealings with the
rental car company Enterprise Rent-A-Car. According to the company's website (www.enterprise.com), as of February 2015 they
are the largest car rental brand in North America and, based on
J.D. Power surveys as of December 2014, are consistently ranked
as the top car rental brand by consumers. Apart from providing
great rates, the obvious difference I see is clearly in the empowerment of Enterprise's employees.

Empowerment plays a major part in them being ranked number one, as even the counter check-in staff are there to make sure
you're completely satisfied. Enterprise staff will make sure you
choose a vehicle you like, based on availability. When you return
the rental vehicle, the first question is usually, "How did you like

your rental?" If the response is in any way negative or even tentative, the staff will immediately try to find ways to rectify your concern on the spot.

I've experienced Enterprise's great service hundreds of times over eight years, and have noticed how different they are from other big brands, whose location staff are not empowered to make decisions and must defer to regional or head offices for a solution or for a later response. At Enterprise, the staff's ability to take care of any customer issue on their own usually defuses the situation immediately, and the client leaves with an incentive or some type of compensation or resolution. More importantly, Enterprise's clients are usually impressed or satisfied that the matter is dealt with quickly and effectively, thus reducing the need for lengthy follow-up calls or emails. This type of empowerment to rectify most customer concerns on the spot maximizes loyalty and referrals to a brand or store location, increasing business considerably.

At the end of the day, the Enterprise difference is the result of well-trained leaders and team members who are accountable and empowered to transform an organization by taking necessary action on the spot. This autonomy leads to employees who are happier and more fulfilled, and that in turn leads to much higher levels of client satisfaction and brand loyalty.

If you observe all of the practices and behaviors we've reviewed in this chapter consistently, you'll go a long way to differentiating yourself and your company with your superior service and an excellent purchase experience for the customer. They will not forget where to go or whom to call next time.

SUMMARY

- **Strive to deliver a great purchase and service experience.**
  While service and pricing are at the top of the list for most

retail and car buyers, the one thing that motivates shoppers to choose one dealer or retailer over the other is a good purchase or dealer experience.

- **Successful individual sales reps and organizations today share one thing in common:** They're good at relationship building, as well as delivering and maintaining a great purchase and/or service experience.

- **Aim to exceed customer expectations.** Clients today are too busy to put up with sub-standard service and most will pay a little more for added convenience and service. Take this as an opportunity to deliver outstanding service to build long-term, raving-fan clients.

- **Add more value than anyone else and you will win more clients.** Value is often misconstrued as offering the lowest price or the biggest discount. But that's far from true in today's marketplace of tech-savvy, informed consumers. You can create and add value in many ways, without focusing on price or discount. Remember value is perceived, so focus on what's important to your client to know what relevant value-adds to offer up.

- **Listen to your client's key needs and desires.** Present an overall value proposition by breaking down any important incentives or perks that your dealership or establishment offers, and defer the element of price until after you've outlined your list of valuable features and benefits.

- **Convenience** is a very big deal for consumers today. Your goal as someone in the sales and service industry is to provide more convenient ways for your clients to appreciate a higher level of satisfaction through positive sales and service experiences with you and your establishment.

- **Service:** What really defines a great dealership or retailer is consistently delivering over-the-top customer service that drives growth through repeat business and referrals.

- **Accountability:** Any sales and service team needs to be held accountable in order to deliver the best overall customer experience. It is in the best interest of ownership and management to have a motivated sales team that is onside and committed to the overall success of the company. Then they are willing to be held to higher levels of accountability in order to deliver a positive purchase or service experience.

- **Management and sales should discuss why accountability is important,** and should support each other to accomplish their greater goals by highlighting the importance of everyone's individual role to the overall success of the team or the organization.

- **Establish clearly defined goals and metrics:** With sales, it's all about the numbers. Management and sales teams must define annual and monthly targets and use metrics to track progress on goals for pending and completed sales, numbers of clients engaged or sales calls made, etc. I recommend that a proven contact management software system be used to track this data.

- **Break down overall dealership or sales team goals into individual targets and keep the sales and service teams accountable.** The key to sales accountability is to translate bigger goals into smaller, bite-sized individual targets. This will help to clarify the individual goals, as well as how to implement them and take action to achieve them.

- **Create a competitive team sales board or individual log of the metrics being measured.** The sales team should record their numbers daily and report them at least weekly during an overall review in a sales meeting. They should also prepare to be challenged. This weekly accountability to the rest of the team creates healthy competition and should help to motivate those who are lagging to catch up, or others to jump out to take the lead.

- **Acknowledge and celebrate accomplishments.** In most automotive and retail sales environments, not enough emphasis is placed on acknowledging sales accomplishments. Accountability and individual drive can quickly dwindle if a sales team or individual is not acknowledged for delivering a consistently great purchase and service experience.

- **Weekly debriefs and feedback during sales meetings build on accountability and responsibility.** This kind of open environment encourages staff to share some of the best ideas on past customer experiences and future opportunities.

- **Empowerment:** One of the most powerful and effective tools available to an employee in any business, empowerment means possessing the resources, motivation, skills and authority to be responsible and accountable for the outcomes of one's own actions while addressing customer issues.

CHAPTER 7

THE ART OF MAKING THE DEAL

Of all aspects of the sales process, this is my favorite. Although the other parts of the process are important, I usually can't wait to sit down with clients in my office to start the negotiating process.

Recently, I had a client refer to the whole negotiation process as an experience in the art of deal making. I could see why he felt this way as there were many variables and factors, both in and out of the dealership's control, that led to him purchasing two vehicles on the same day and subsequently referring many other clients thereafter. He was fascinated with the various avenues I was willing to explore to make his deals happen.

It's a fact that some clients in today's information age will know more than their salesperson about the products or models because they have done their homework. Regardless of their exposure or access to information, you cannot allow clients to out-negotiate you in making deals on your turf. You simply need to be better prepared with your negotiating skills and style when it comes down to deal making.

To make the best deals possible, there are some fundamental steps you will need to master. Some of these steps have been covered in detail in chapter 2, Eight Principles for a Successful (Sales) Career, and chapter 3, Best Practices of Top Sales Performers.

I've summarized the following keys to the art of deal making, based on my twenty-five years of sales experience. Some may seem outlandish or unnecessary, but I assure you they are all critical to building trust and making many sales.

THE GREETING: STARTING OFF ON THE RIGHT FOOT

Greet your prospect with genuine interest and a positive attitude to assure them that you'll be their ultimate guide to solving their purchasing needs. As discussed in chapters 1 and 2, the foundation for negotiating, building trust, and deal making starts with your initial greeting, by establishing common ground.

Your greeting must be delivered with a positive attitude and the clear intention to do this consistently every time. Then right from the start, your chances are significantly greater of closing because your good intentions will be transparent to your clients and they will know they can start trusting your guidance.

Remember, clients are shopping for a salesperson more than (or as much as) they're shopping for a product, so the quality and authenticity of the personal connection you make with them will be a key factor in their decision.

FOLLOW A DISCIPLINED PROCESS

Respect your potential client's time and they will respect yours. You can establish this mind-set right away by thanking them for making the visit to your location, or for initiating or returning a sales call. Clients want to make deals with professionals who are good listeners and can respect their time by being organized.

They seek sales professionals who can resolve or negotiate a solution within a reasonable time.

Deal making and negotiations are as much about process and progress as they are about price. The negotiations start from very early on; in the initial stages you should be listening closely to what your client is looking for and making mental notes of key hints the potential client provides. To negotiate and close a deal in a timely manner would mean satisfying most (if not all) the needs and objectives relevant to your client and giving them the personal attention and time needed to negotiate a resolution.

Deal making and negotiations are as much about process and progress as they are about price.

Often times you may not have an immediate solution and you may need to do some research; in that case, always make a list of your prospective client's key objectives and the details relevant to them, and follow up with a phone call or email within a preset time frame. In other words, if you do need to follow up, always set the next connection time; for example, "Mr. Jones, I will gather these details and will email or call you back within an hour" (or whatever the agreed upon timeframe is).

Remember, buying is emotional, so don't risk frustrating your customers by procrastinating or inadvertently delaying your response; set a specific timeframe, get back to them by then, and be prepared.

QUALIFYING YOUR LEADS AND PROSPECTS

This is a significant part of the sales process and how well you handle it will ultimately affect your success. You should consistently follow a step-by-step qualifying process, including everything from where and how to get leads, what to say or ask when you have them and, finally, how to close them.

In the retail sales profession, leads and prospects come in many forms so preparation and readiness are vital. Leads can be from direct showroom traffic, sales calls, the Internet, referrals, repeat business, community events, service departments and many other avenues. Identifying the source of your leads matters as this gives clues to the best qualifying questions to ask.

Identifying the source of your leads matters as this gives clues to the best qualifying questions to ask.

For example, if someone is a repeat client, they're already familiar with your facility, your products and they may already have a comfort level in dealing with you and your establishment. The qualifying questions you ask these clients will be somewhat different from those you ask a first-time visitor to your showroom, even though they may end up purchasing the same model or product.

The qualifying process is different for each individual, so it's important to ask high-value qualifying questions, as listed previously in chapter 3 and expanded on here in no particular order.

- **Question:** *Will you be using the vehicle more for work or routine, everyday family needs?*
  Reason: The client feedback here will enlighten you on the key uses of the vehicle, whether it's for a large or small family, how much cargo room is needed (i.e., for kids' sports bags, or for work samples). Is it a lifestyle change where the buyer wants a sports car now that he/she is an empty nester, or an all-wheel-drive SUV for cottage life or skiing? Qualifying questions like this narrow down the search criteria to specific models in a timely and intelligent manner.

- **Question:** *Is there anything that would keep you from making a purchasing decision today?*
  Reason: You are probing to uncover any objections that would hinder a commitment today. Sometimes all the decision makers are not present. This may then direct you to try impressing the one person in front of you so they're excited to tell the other party about their positive experience, and that they both need to come back to see you instead of the competition. Regardless of the answer, you're able to establish a timeline as to when a deal may be possible, thus allowing you to strategize accordingly to create urgency. You should keep this in mind for when you sit with the client after your presentation and demo; for example, pointing out a time-limited offer on available incentives or limited product availability can create a sense of urgency.

- **Question:** *What's the current mileage on your present vehicle? Are you planning on doing similar mileage or have your circumstances changed?*
  Reason: To determine driving habits and how best to guide the client and structure the deal. This question also lends consideration to fuel economy and maintenance costs, a need for winter tires and extended warranty recommendations. Again, keep listening for key clues in response to this qualifying question that you can use later when negotiating.

- **Question:** *What research and comparisons have you done online?*
  Reason: The days of clients coming blind to a retailer's showroom without first doing their own research are over. Be prepared that your potential new client may have

pointed questions about your products and services, so it
may be necessary to ask some pointed questions of them.
Asking this question up front in your qualifying process
reveals your customer's level of preparedness, seriousness
and their intended timeline for purchasing your product or
service. If the client appears to have done in-depth research
and is very specific in answering questions and referring
to packages, options, colors, incentive programs and so on,
you will want to proceed more quickly through qualifying
compared to someone who requires more guidance and
who may be less prepared. Some clients are so prepared
that they may have already shortlisted or settled on your
model(s) as a potential choice, so don't prolong the process
any more than is required. In cases where a client has done
a great deal of research already, efficiency and clarity from
you are important.

- **Question:** *What are the key criteria that must be satisfied
  for you to make your new purchase decision?*
  Reason: This pointed question helps to narrow down the
  qualification process to specific needs. Your potential
  client will suggest a wide range of requirements, including payments, budget, age or model year range, financial
  preference (cash, finance or lease), trade-in value, and
  desired features. Some clients may also refer to features
  they no longer require, such as passenger capacity now
  that kids are grown, or lower or higher mileage limits as a
  result of changes in work requirements (such as working
  from home). Although your client is giving you all kinds
  of information about what they are looking for in a vehicle, you need to ask this question to find out what features
  and needs are critical to them rather than nice-to-have.
  For example, things like a speedy delivery date may also

be an important criterion as some clients have a need for immediate delivery due to an accident, mechanical issues, or the need to move.

- **Question:** *Have you thought about an alternative such as . . . ?*
  Reason: When you offer alternatives, you may be able to point out options that the client hadn't considered; or, more importantly, learning about alternatives may reaffirm the client's preference or selection. Clients usually welcome valued opinions and alternatives, so don't hesitate to make suggestions after listening to their needs. Those suggestions don't have to be restricted to other products and models; they could also include offering grounded or factory demos, clear-out models offering bigger value and savings, or multiple security deposits.

- **Question:** *What concerns do you have, if any, about moving forward?*
  Reason: This qualifying question may flush out any other lingering objections or concerns and it clears the way to negotiations. Remember, every concern or objection you handle moves you closer to a potential deal. Asking this question indicates to your clients that their needs matter, and that you want to make sure they've been addressed adequately. This builds confidence for them to share with you their real underlying issues, thus paving the way to a deal.

- **Question:** *What made you decide to look at and consider our product?*
  Reason: This question is intended to discover what attracted them to come in today. Were they just passing

by? Were they referred by another client with a similar
product? Was it advertising, incentives, product research
that motivated them to come in? These questions will
help to guide your approach to the deal. If the client was
a referral, there's usually a better chance of closing them,
given that a friend or existing client has already endorsed
you, the product and your establishment.

- **Question:** *Are you familiar with our dealership and
  our high-value philosophy?*
  Reason: A client new to your establishment is likely not
  familiar with all the benefits of doing business with you.
  This question provides an opening to establish and build
  value that separates you from the competition. Asking
  this high-value question allows you to better quantify and
  establish a level of trust, differentiate your product and
  service from the competition and offer up more relevant
  features and benefits, thus satisfying more clients and
  closing more deals. If you advance to the client a better
  value proposition than the competition, they will leave
  strongly considering your product because you've educated them and provided more value and comfort.

- **Question:** *Are you aware of all the benefits of doing
  business with us?*
  Reason: Simply by asking and answering this question,
  you can easily establish additional value for your client
  by making them aware of other benefits of dealing with
  you and your establishment rather than the competition,
  beyond the value of the product they are purchasing
  (even something as simple as free lifetime replacement of
  remote key batteries). Other additional benefits could be
  an in-house loyalty program with additional savings based

on service visits, or exclusive member clubs with special invitations to all-expenses-paid events.

It is up to you to know and present the benefits of your value proposition, as they vary from location to location. Know that not all value-added features and benefits are relevant to all clients; listen carefully after asking this qualifying question and others, and elaborate more on what matters to each specific client.

- **Question:** *Are you familiar with or aware of all the recent awards, consumer reports, rankings or safety standards of the model you're interested in and how it compares to the competition?*

  Reason: This is another question that attempts to find out how much research the client may have done and how much knowledge they have of your product. Some manufacturers, like Lexus, Toyota and Honda, have long-standing reputations based on reliability, durability and higher resale values. Is the client familiar with the strength of your brand, or with safety rankings compared to the competition? Use key product comparisons such as consumer reports to substantiate these claims, to build value and to ask for the order.

- **Question:** *Have you read the recent consumer reports? If not, let me show you what other satisfied consumers are saying.*

  Reason: If you have products or models of vehicles that rank well in consumer reports you should show them off to prospective buyers. These particular rankings are usually unbiased, direct feedback from thousands of clients who've already used the product. What better source to use than other satisfied clients?

- **Question:** *Will you be trading in your present vehicle and what have you enjoyed most about it?*
  Reason: You certainly want to know if there's a potential trade-in right away, as it will affect the structure of the transaction significantly. Probe your prospect to speak about how they've enjoyed their current vehicle and find out what features they've liked and disliked before you decide what features and benefits to focus on in your presentation. Learning about your customer's emotional connection to their current vehicle helps you to build a value proposition and will go a long way towards helping you make a new deal.

- **Question:** *Are you aware of the incentives available for you this week or this month?*
  Reason: If the answer is yes and the client was prompted to come in thanks to a recent sale or promotion, it means they've responded favorably to the promotion and you have an interested client. If the answer is no, you have a big opportunity to create some excitement by advising them what deals are available today! Either way you have great potential.

- **Question:** *What led you to call or visit us today?*
  Reason: Establish whether the client was drawn to your retail establishment or dealership by advertising or marketing campaigns, location or proximity to work, etc. You want to know the source of your leads at all times. Focusing on what led them to call or visit can help with future marketing and advertising campaigns; this information can also guide you to further details about the client's shopping habits and clues to hot-button items at the heart of a potential deal.

- **Question:** *What are the keys factors for you in making a decision today or very soon?*
  Reason: Similar to the previous point, now that the client is in your showroom or on the phone discussing specifics about the product, you will want to find out the client's real hot buttons, those essential items that must be fulfilled to close a deal. Those essential factors could include: a need for all-wheel drive, fuel efficiency, availability, payment budget, trade value, delivery time and date and available incentives. Addressing the client's list of key factors one by one will ultimately lead to an offer and possibly a deal.

THE PRESENTATION

From the greeting stage through till now, your time spent with the client should be building trust, excitement and comfort in dealing with you. Now it's time to proceed with a presentation of your product, in this case an automobile. Your presentation should be concise and designed to inspire, enlighten and impress; it should back up the high-value qualifying questions you've asked previously by reinforcing features and value-adds you've discovered are important to your client.

Your presentation should not exceed fifteen minutes if you've done proper qualifying. You can always recap a bit more after the test drive, but for now keep moving the process along to keep the client engaged and maintain control of the process yourself instead of the client dictating which way to go next.

Now that you've asked the high-value questions, it's time to first clarify the issues, and then focus on presenting to the customer's key areas of interest. This helps your client to see further value in the product and to develop more trust in you. In fact, all presentations should be adapted to the client's situation and should begin with a short recap of relevant items. Your actual presentation should be separated into three key parts:

1. The product presentation
2. The demonstration
3. The presentation of numbers and deal options

Product Presentation

Here are some key product presentation points that you can elaborate upon. Which points you choose to focus on and emphasize will depend on the individual client's specific needs and wants, revealed by your qualifying questions:

- **Safety features:** In today's ultra-competitive marketplace, high-tech safety features are becoming more commonplace as standard features in most cars and are influencing more and more buying decisions. Some clients are even narrowing down their purchase decision before ever visiting a showroom, researching and choosing vehicles with certain safety criteria essential to them and that fit within their budget. Twenty years ago, just one or two airbags and side crumple zones were considered big selling features. Today, we're comparing safety technology with ten or more airbags, including knee and rear glass locations, and advanced safety technology options, such as rear cross traffic alert, blind spot monitors and night vision just to name a few. Present safety features of specific interest to your customer first, then elaborate and impress with others that you feel are relevant, to build more value against the competition and to inspire your client.

- **Cargo capacity:** Clients today can recite dimensions and stats like never before, and cargo capacity can be a major factor in making a final decision. I recently sold a Lexus SUV largely on the fact that it could accommodate skis inside the cabin with its 40/20/40 split rear seat arrangement, while still carrying four adults. This was important to my client; that one major convenience closed the deal. It's important to realize the full potential and flexibility of cargo areas in all your models as customers seek more and more versatility today. Listening to and understanding customer needs is key to your presentation.

- **Performance:** This will always be a factor to most car buyers, so it's important to know key performance data of all models compared to the competition, such as horsepower, torque, engine displacement and number of cylinders. Many car buying decisions are made based on performance due to individual driving habits; be educated and prepared to make your case effectively.

- **Fuel efficiency:** Fuel efficiency is another key factor influencing buyers' final decisions because it affects overall operating costs. Fuel consumption ratings and fuel grade requirements are increasingly becoming routine considerations in every purchase decision. For example, some clients' questions are specific to whether particular models will perform on regular gas to avoid paying premium fuel prices. You need to know the answers to these questions or have fuel guide references available at all times, and be able to quantify your ratings compared to the competition. Many car buying decisions are being made today based on cost advantages associated with fuel efficiency or the ability to use regular grade fuel.

- **Passenger comfort:** Focus on key features that scream comfort. In today's modern cars, comfort comes in all sorts of fancy features: heated rear passenger seats, heated steering wheel, powered tilt and telescopic steering, ventilated seats and multi-zone climate control systems to name a few. There's also a focus on long-distance driving comfort as it relates to overall room and dimensions such as headroom, legroom and ease of entry and exit. With such a wide variety of models to choose from and compete against, knowing how to present your value packages and comfort features will win you more deals.

- **Handling and maneuverability:** Most of the handling and performance capabilities will be demonstrated or experienced during a test drive, but point out in your presentation any key handling characteristics and features that seem relevant to your client's needs, such as adaptive or tuned suspension, wheel sizes, steering type and transmission configuration (i.e., seven or eight speeds).

To recap, make sure that your presentation is tailored to go into more depth on key areas of interest to your client, and spend less time on areas of less interest. Your presentation should not be a boring A-Z catalogue of every feature, but more of an enlightenment on hot button areas that your client cares about plus relevant points that you deem important based on your client's feedback. In short, know how to properly position your product during the presentation. Present with a focus on the client and be prepared for objections, questions and interruptions.

The Demonstration

If you've gone through a proper qualifying and presentation process, then the demo drive will be more meaningful and complete because you'll already be aware of the features important to your client and of the characteristics worth elaborating on during the test drive.

The purchase of a car is often driven by emotion and less out of necessity. The benefits you discuss in an enlightened presentation appeal to the customer's rational side; the test drive not only reinforces your presentation, but can also play to that buyer's emotional side, connecting them emotionally to the car and moving them mentally closer to ownership and a deal.

During the test drive, you want to enhance the buyer's experience with a strategic demonstration, including a well thought out route that allows you to show off the car's cornering, acceleration and handling characteristics on city streets and highways. Planning the test drive carefully in advance is aimed at making the consumer feel attached and excited about their potential purchase.

Your test drive and demonstration should last about twenty minutes, keeping your client excited throughout the process so they are ready to move on to the next major step: sitting down to explore pricing and options to acquire the vehicle.

Setting up the Potential Deal

I find this step to be more of a necessity today than in previous years as many dealerships and retailers try to level the competitive playing field by offering the same types of ultra-modern facilities and perks, all aimed at enhancing the purchase and service experience. Remember, a key differentiator—and a big factor in the purchase decision—is you, and the value you add personally to the client's experience.

Now that you've completed your presentation and test drive and are back at the dealership, this is the time to take a moment and remind them briefly, just before you sit down at your desk, why they should do business with you rather than the competition. This small step will be valuable in the negotiations because your potential customers will soon realize that they're not just buying a car or a product but also buying into an organization full of service, support and perks.

Remember, a key differentiator—and a big factor in the purchase decision—is you, and the value you add personally to the client's experience.

As discussed in chapter 2, Eight Principles for a Successful (Sales) Career, highlight briefly the key conveniences of the product and outline additional perks associated with doing business with you. This is all aimed at substantiating more overall value in a relationship with you because you enlightened them; differentiated yourself, your product and your dealership; and conveyed a more complete purchase and service experience.

Negotiating the Deal

In today's sales environment, clients come into a showroom with the perception of having to battle to make a deal. That may be based on past or recent experiences, stereotypes, or they may have a heightened sense of apprehension because they are inexperienced with purchasing cars. No matter what the reason, potential customers often visit a showroom with their backs up, anticipating a lengthy, difficult negotiation. Although they have full access to product and service information via the Internet and social media, many clients will expect to experience a less-than-straightforward buying process.

This is where the opportunity lies for you to shine and make a huge difference by exceeding their expectations and delivering the opposite experience of what they're expecting. You accomplish this by following all the normal steps in an effective sales process (such as the greeting, qualifying, demonstrating, as previously discussed), but also genuinely showing concern that your client stays within budget and purchases the best vehicle or product for their needs—all while making the negotiation process clear and understandable.

Conveying this information effectively puts you in a stronger position to make recommendations that suit your customer—recommendations that may even be more profitable for you as well. Your customers are actually looking for advice and counsel from you because you are the expert in this field. Your ability to answer finance- and lease-related questions, for example, and to arrive at a suitable price or payments within a reasonable time will leave them with comfort and clarity. Everything you do throughout the sales process helps your clients to move towards ultimately making a deal.

So it's important to be prepared, listen to and address attentively all the concerns as you go through the process. Closing is a by-product of doing all the little steps above and results from positioning yourself well to gain the buyer's confidence, to justify value, and to make recommendations—earning the right to assume and ask for the sale.

You want your potential clients to know that you'll be patient throughout the process, that you've been listening to their concerns all along and are working to structure a deal that suits them. I can't stress enough that listening to what their needs are and sharing in their emotion will make them feel comfortable to work with you, and to give and take to come to a deal.

Closing is a by-product of doing all the little steps
in the selling process and results from positioning yourself
well to gain the buyer's confidence, to justify value,
and to make recommendations—earning the right
to assume and ask for the sale.

Remember, from the second you meet the potential client, each step strategically involves a bit of closing by successfully transitioning you and the buyer through the process.

Here are some keys points to prepare you for making your best deal:

- **Always sit down to negotiate:** It's a formal process, so sit down with your clients and offer refreshments to slow them down. You've made it this far and have laid valuable groundwork; so don't blow your deal by being a casual negotiator.

- **Make notes to recap:** Write a short list of important points covered in the process so far. This will show the client that you're taking their main concerns seriously. While you're at it, ask if there are any other key criteria you've missed, to further engage the client and to continue to show interest in addressing their needs.

- **Give your full attention:** I once lost a deal for this very reason. I had test driven three different cars with this potential client and when we sat down to review numbers, my phone and email devices kept going off and I became distracted, even though I tried to ignore them. The client later made a point of telling me that the distraction had turned them off because it appeared I wasn't focused on them. Lesson learned: Even if the clients themselves are using their devices, don't allow yourself such distractions.

- **Review and select models and options of interest for pricing:** Now that you've recapped important details with the client and they have your full attention, it's time to outline their selection of models. This is where you're landing them on a particular vehicle and package and are itemizing any additional options, protection items, warranties, etc., based on their feedback and your professional recommendations. Remember to outline substantive value so price does not become the main issue.

- **If a trade is involved, have it evaluated at this point while seated:** You should know by now if there is a trade-in, having addressed that question in your qualifying process. But before you go any further on final quotes, enquire again if a trade is part of the deal. Asking again will make sure you avoid any last-minute surprises; it will also keep you in charge of the process and the clients will appreciate that you have a system.

  Having a trade-in can often work to your advantage if you structure the deal right, so get all the cards on the table to give yourself and the client the best possible options. A trade-in, if financed or owned, can provide additional tax savings on cash, finance and lease deals. In some cases with Toyota and Lexus, the equity can be used with leases as multiple security deposits, to reduce interest rates and the total overall costs. So getting all the negotiating parameters on the table will help you to better advise the client on options and how to structure the deal while continuing to build trust.

- **Build and present quotes based on financial preference:** Present at least two prices or payment options to start the number crunching process. The goal is to narrow down towards a final selection based on factors like budget, value-added options included, total budget for price or payment—all of which were previously discussed in your qualifying and discovery. Once you present numbers and associated options, the client's reaction is usually automatic. They will most likely suggest the numbers you have offered are above their budget. Don't be alarmed. First, this is their way of engaging in the negotiation process. And this feedback is exactly what you want as it indicates some of the main objections from which to negotiate, or at the least a starting point.

Objections and quality feedback relating to payment, price or overall budget are automatic for most clients. But keep in mind most customers have already done pricing online, so it's really no surprise to them even though clients may pretend otherwise. Don't get caught up in or discouraged by the objections; start sifting through where they're really coming from and ultimately where the client would like to end up with price or payment. At the end of this step, you and your prospective client should be clear on exactly what model and options they want, plus what the key criteria are for making a mutual deal.

- **Use your negotiating tools to close the deal:** Negotiating in the retail and automotive world today is more about providing credible recommendations and advice, building trust and solutions-based selling, rather than just price and discounts. You don't have to give a client exactly what they say they want in terms of price, because often times that may not be their best solution. Today's busy clientele appreciates alternatives and enlightenment about options. Knowing what options to present with assertiveness and confidence will strengthen your negotiating position, gain their trust and empower you to ask for and make the deal—and to be more profitable.

- **The final steps to closing the deal:** So far, you've covered all the necessary steps and have presented different options and value scenarios, payment and pricing, and you have now settled on a car. It's time to conclude the deal. Whether or not a client has made it clear to you that he or she is not ready to buy today, after all the work you've done to this point, you must ask for the business today! As long as a client is still seated in your office and engaged with you, there's a potential deal there, so subtly ask for it after each major step, and maintain control of the process.

Here are some effective closing questions to get the offer and the deal:

- Have we settled on a vehicle or model you'd be very happy with?
- Have we included all the features and options that are important to you?
- Are you happy with silver or gray? Are there any other color preferences that you'd say yes to today?
- Now that we've covered all the important factors in making this choice, what's the ideal scenario in which you could sign or say yes today?
- Mr. Jones, we've chosen carefully and covered every aspect of this purchase that's important to you. Now let me show you how to make it work within your budget and get you this vehicle today!
- You've made a great choice in this model and package with all the valuable options included. Now let's help you make the choice to purchase today. I will show you how easy owning this vehicle can be.

- Mr. Jones, you seem excited about the possibility of driving this vehicle every day. I will show you some great financial options to make this happen today.
- Tell me, Mr. Jones, what we need to work on together to make this deal happen for you today?
- Now that you've selected the right car, tell me whether you prefer leasing or financing options to make your best deal today?

These types of high-value questions can be effective in getting an offer or commitment from your client. Most auto deals do not require heavy sales tactics or vigorous negotiations at all, as long as you've set the expectations from the beginning, as explained earlier.

Offers can come from clients and deals can be made easier by first strategically outlining any incentives available and how they relate to your specific case. Remember, your potential buyers may have already done extensive research so don't assume they're not aware of the available incentives or programs. Once you've presented your value proposition relative to the model being sought, you should then always wait for a response. This response will be a key indicator of what the client is thinking in terms of making a deal. For example, they may ask or suggest the following:

- That's the manufacturer's incentive available to anyone; what else is available from the dealership?
- What can you do for me over and above what you've outlined?
- My budget is a bit below that and I was hoping to be at this number monthly or a certain total price.

When you hear any such feedback from your client after you've asked the types of closing questions outlined earlier in this chapter, you're on your way to getting an offer. Then it's up to you listen carefully to the clues that you should react to in order to make a deal.

Now that we've covered the deal making process, it's important to remember that it's relatively simple. And the more prepared you are, the simpler and easier it is. My sales success has always been based on simplicity. I'm often asked by clients, "Is it that easy?" And my answer is, "Why reinvent the wheel or why complicate things?"

Value, product, service and relationship building are all important parts of making a deal, so listen to and focus on the client's needs to structure the best deal and exceed their expectations.

SUMMARY

- **Greet your prospects with genuine interest and a positive attitude;** assure them you'll be their ultimate guide to solving their purchasing needs. This is your big chance to make an impact right from the get-go, so don't blow it with a lackluster welcome. Be enthusiastic and genuine.

- **Respect your potential client's time and they will respect yours.** You can establish respect right away by thanking them for making the visit to your location or initiating or returning a sales call. Clients want to make deals with other professionals who are good listeners and who respect their time by being organized.

- **Qualify your leads and prospects:** This key part of the sales process can contribute significantly to your ultimate success with many clients. You should follow a consistent, step-by-step process to determine where and how to get leads, what to say or ask when you have them, how you will guide them to make their selection and, finally, how to close them.

- **The Presentation:** From the greeting stage until it's time to make a presentation, your time spent with the client should be building trust so they can be comfortable dealing with you. Your presentation should be designed to inspire, enlighten and impress, and to reinforce the high-value qualifying questions you've asked previously.

- **Demonstration:** If you've gone through a proper qualifying and presentation process, then the demo drive will be more meaningful and complete because you'll be aware of what features are most important to focus on during the test drive. This is also a great time to continue building rapport and trust so when you return from the demo drive you're more in control to guide them further through the process and improve your chances of making a deal.

- **Setting up the potential deal:** Once you've completed your presentation and test drive and are back at the dealership, it's time to briefly remind your client of the value of doing business with you and your establishment before sitting down at your desk.

- **Negotiating the deal:** In today's sales environment clients come into a showroom expecting a less than straightforward buying process, and with the perception of having to battle to make a deal. But this is where your opportunity lies to shine and make a huge difference by exceeding expectations, and by delivering a sales experience that's completely the opposite of what they were expecting.

- **Key Points to Prepare for Closing the Deal:**
  - Always sit down to negotiate.
  - Make notes to recap and engage the client.
  - Give your full attention.

- Review and select models and options of interest for pricing.
- If a trade is involved, have it evaluated at this point to have all relevant details and to avoid surprises.
- Build and present quotes based on financial preference.

- **Use Your Negotiating Tools to Close:** Negotiating in the retail and automotive world today is about giving credible recommendations and advice, building trust with the client and solutions-based selling, rather than just price and discounts. So use all the negotiating tools available to you to close the deal.

CHAPTER 8

SUPPORT TOOLS AND STRATEGIES

The key to success in sales, as in most aspects of business, lies largely in innovation, marketing and resourcefulness, as mentioned earlier in chapter 5. Of course you need to know your stuff and be prepared, but being resourceful and seeking support from others can make all the difference, taking you over the top from mediocre results to being a top performer.

Resourceful individuals can always find ways to maximize outcomes and to top sales charts because they create their own opportunities; they don't wait for them to happen. Many people have access to great resources but never use them to maximize their potential.

In sales, opportunities are always around you and the key is to keep an open mind to possibilities and finding good prospects that others fail to. Resourceful sales reps will work directly with their clients, finding creative ways to problem solve and win the deal. To win even more deals, I encourage you to maximize your full potential and exceed even your own expectations by learning

about and using all the tools and support available to you within
your dealership or sales organization.

After twenty-five years of selling all across North America, in
advertising and automotive retail, I've summed up the following
key ways you can maximize the resources available to you daily
to become a top performer.

ESTABLISH SUPPORT

The strength of any organization lies in people, because together
everyone achieves more. Use the existing support team around
you to your own benefit, and to enhance and maximize the overall potential of your establishment. A salesperson should always
know when and where to seek help and objective insight from a
personal network of professionals, team members and managers.
Sharing experiences and ideas has always been a practical method of obtaining support from the right people; and if you choose
the right people, it can also be fun.

Work with the people who are already around you to create
innovative solutions that win more business. This can include
leaning on each other for product information, sharing ideas
and experiences, closing tips, and assisting with client services
through teamwork. Whom you spend time with is often who you
become, so choose people who are better than you at specific
tasks and roles; being around them will help you to elevate your
own standards more quickly, by following their example and
learning from one-on-one interaction with them.

Whom you spend time with is often who you become,
so choose people who are better than you at specific
tasks and roles; being around them will help you
to elevate your own standards.

Good managers can and should be your best source of support, providing motivation and leadership by example, instead of being bossy and ignorant.

A good sales manager or team manager is really only effective if he or she is focused on team building, solutions, innovation, marketing, and support and not just on a title. I've witnessed managers who consistently choose ignorance over intellect and who show a lack of urgency when sales staff approach them for guidance, advice, appraisals and support—even while clients are present. I've never understood how a business spends so much on advertising and marketing, and then when the clients come through the doors the staff, including managers, are not perked up and ready to make the sales process more efficient. All managers and support staff should be alert, focused and standing by to provide immediate assistance when necessary.

INTERNAL SUPPORT

Within larger organizations, you will find many departments available to support and complement the sales function; in a dealership, for example, there might be service, parts, business development, Internet sales and others. However, the majority of internal cooperation and support is largely between the sales, service and parts departments.

Even though these are separate departments, each with individual goals and targets, they should all be united in the common goal of ultimate customer satisfaction. I'm baffled almost daily by the lack of genuine cooperation and support these various departments often show towards each other. Companies and managers often preach the gospel that all departments should work together to create the best customer experience possible, but rarely do they practice their daily interactions in the business with this goal in mind.

I've criticized this lack of cohesiveness between departments for many years, as if often leads to customer dissatisfaction and lower employee morale.

Interdepartmental Challenges and Support Solutions

Here are some everyday challenges to watch for between departments and potential support solutions to overcome them:

- **Handling interdepartmental issues relating to particular customer concerns while in the client's presence.** If interdepartmental issues come up when dealing with client concerns, they should never be handled in front of the clients. Openly discussing conflict or disagreement between departments in front of clients is not just bad customer service, it also gives clients the overall negative impression that the dealership or business is highly disorganized, dysfunctional, and lacks cohesiveness.

  Solution: Just as you should always sit down to negotiate a deal, you should always discuss and work out client solutions behind closed doors. Present the client with solutions or options after you have had the internal discussion.

- **Varying standards and support for different departments.** Ideally, every department should be held to the same standard and given the same level of support. That is, every department in an organization should be held just as accountable as the next for the level of productivity and the quality they each deliver before the product or service is turned over to the next department or delivered to the client. However, the reality is that there are often widely varying standards of performance for different departments, which leads to reduced productivity and lack of efficiency every day.

In particular, the sales department in an auto dealership is generally held to much higher standards than all the other departments, including detailing, service and parts. As a result, no matter how hard sales works to please customers and close sales, a lack of effort or accountability in another department can work against the goal of creating an excellent customer experience.

A great and all too common example of this double standard is when a sales rep has done their job and the client is excited to take delivery of the product, whether new or used, and the vehicle first goes to detailing to be prepared for presentation to the customer. But often these vehicles are turned over to be delivered with a substandard detailing job having been done.

If the detailing department is held to lower standards and has no real accountability, this last step in the sales process can leave the customer with a negative impression, undermining all the careful work that was done by sales earlier to make them happy and satisfied.

Solution: Consistent quality control measures and levels of accountability and support across the organization are integral to delivering the best possible product and providing the best possible service at all times. There's no point attempting to assist another colleague or department unless your goal is to deliver as good a job as they are expected to do—or better.

When it comes to seeking internal support, your best resources are usually other team members, so identify the strengths and

specialties of your teammates, including other managers, and share
expertise among yourselves to maximize everyone's effectiveness.
In my current sales environment, I approach different team members for technical product information or evaluations because each
of them is more proficient in their knowledge of individual models.

USE THE ASSETS AVAILABLE TO YOU

Similar to sharing strengths and responsibilities with your teammates and managers, find creative ways to utilize simple assets
that are already available to you within your dealership and sales
organization. Often times the solutions are right there for you,
so you don't always have to reinvent the wheel. For example, as
discussed in chapter 6, sharing ideas in sales meetings is a simple
and resourceful way to leverage an existing forum to improve
how you do your job; the entire sales team learns from each other,
generating tips, answers and clues for all to use.

Using your physical facility to your advantage in dealing
with clients is another simple way to turn existing assets into
value-added benefits that can help you close a sale. Always start
by making your potential and existing clients feel welcome by
offering refreshments every time you meet with them even if it's
just a glass of water or a cup of coffee to slow them down, and to
engage them. Always make them feel right at home and comfortable while waiting or working with you so they can be relaxed
and you can point out all the available amenities, such as the
refreshment area, restrooms and lounges.

You should always present your facility and the value-added
conveniences it offers, such as free Wi-Fi, work stations, electrical
outlets, etc. These are all simple, useable resources, but don't take
them for granted. Leverage them with your clients, bringing them
to their attention to build customer comfort and create value while
ultimately leading to new sales, referrals and customer loyalty.

USE TECHNOLOGY TO YOUR ADVANTAGE

No matter where you work, your dealership will have invested in technology to run and support the business. Use those technology assets and tools to your advantage, as resources to help you work smarter and not harder, and to educate yourself.

Today, many retail establishments have online access and specific software customized to do almost everything you need to further your knowledge and experience. Few salespeople use these resources and most are not even aware of the potential wealth of tools and capabilities available at their fingertips. I can attest to this based on my current direct involvement with two dealerships, and with focus groups involving many other dealerships. They all had major customer management software tools available but most of the sales staff were unaware of them, or inexperienced in using them. Many salespeople couldn't even access their own database of clients to find additional untapped leads.

For a sales team to be successful, they must work smarter by utilizing all available tools to continuously educate themselves and to stay current with market and technology trends. Visit relevant websites, sign up to receive e-newsletters and engage in forums that specialize in your product or your field to keep up-to-date on all aspects of your industry.

EXISTING CLIENTS CAN BE YOUR BEST RESOURCE

Clients always appreciate dealing with other professionals, and when you earn their respect they can also be a great resource and source of information for you.

- Existing clients who appreciate dealing with you and have a positive experience with you and your organization will refer other clients and professionals to you.

- Existing clients have expertise in their own field and can provide new ideas and solutions from their experience by referring you to technology, websites, books, networking clubs, sports teams, etc. Don't forget that your clients can become an important part of your professional network and you have much to learn from one another.

ANYTHING'S POSSIBLE

Resourcefulness comes from necessity, your innate creativity and your persistence in striving to be the best you can be at whatever you choose to do. First, adopt the philosophy of possibility.

Top producers find many ways to be resourceful:

- They bring new ideas to the table constantly.
- They have a consistent sales strategy that includes a research action plan, a calling/contact plan, and appropriate follow-up strategies.
- They constantly ask the right high-value questions, not only of customers but also of peers.
- They know how to properly position their products and services against the competition to strengthen their position and to benefit the client.
- They know how and where to search for new and existing untapped leads.
- They are excellent networkers and are not afraid to engage others to help them spread their wings.

ALWAYS HAVE BACK-UP

All sales organizations and sales reps should have back-up documentation readily available to support claims about their products. Testimonials, case studies, endorsements and product research make great additional reference resources to use and present to clients when needed. It's a good idea to have a computer file or binder handy for quick reference.

The world of the sales professional continues to change, and continues to demand more innovative thinking and creativity. In order to compete and to succeed in sales today, salespeople must bring creativity, skills, imagination and the support of other resources to benefit themselves, their organizations and their customers.

SUMMARY

- **Resourceful individuals can always find ways to maximize outcomes** because their mind-set is geared to creating their own opportunities, rather than waiting for things to happen.

- **Resourceful sales reps will work directly with their clients** to solve problems and highlight competitive advantages to win the deal.

- **Resourceful sales reps utilize self-discipline and imagination**, particularly useful in difficult situations.

- **Use the support team around you** to your benefit and to maximize the overall potential of your establishment. The strength of any organization lies in its people, and by working together, everyone achieves more.

- **Internal departments must step up their level of cooperation with each other;** avoid the bickering or internal discussions in front of clients.

- **Raise individual and department standards** to increase productivity and improve the internal support structure.

- **Consistent quality control measures and accountability** are integral to providing effective internal support, and to delivering the best possible product or service at all times.

- **Existing clients are also a good resource tool.** Clients always appreciate dealing with other professionals, and can be another great source of information and support.

- **Resourcefulness comes from necessity, creativity and the persistence** to achieve the most you can at whatever you choose to do by first adopting the philosophy of possibility.

- **Use the assets available to you.** You can utilize simple, everyday assets in your organization to your advantage, like the size of inventory to choose from, or creative thank-you gifts available through your dealership and sales organization.

- **Use technology assets as resources to work smarter and not harder.** In today's modern sales environment, many retail establishments have online access and specific software customized to offer almost everything you need to further your knowledge and experience.

- **Top producers always find ways to bring new ideas to the table.** They do a lot of the little things well, and they never stop finding ways to be better.

- **Always have back-up:** All sales organizations and sales reps need back-up, such as case studies and surveys, to substantiate their claims when needed.

CHAPTER 9

EFFECTIVE TELEPHONE AND EMAIL COMMUNICATION STRATEGIES

In chapter 3, Best Practices of Top Sales Performers, I briefly discussed having a clearly defined purpose when making sales calls or follow-up calls, and an expected outcome prior to initiating a call. In this chapter, I'll break down some of the fundamental steps and strategies for sending successful emails, leaving effective voicemails, and making productive follow-up and prospecting phone calls.

This may all sound like trivial stuff, but clear, polished communications are critical to sales success. The more effective you are as a communicator, the easier it will be to build trust with your clients, the smoother the sales process will go for everyone, and the higher your chances of closing deals and becoming a top performer. Every chance you get to communicate, no matter how small or how seemingly insignificant the subject, is an opportunity to set yourself apart from others and to differentiate yourself as an accomplished professional who's easy to do business with.

EFFECTIVE EMAIL STRATEGIES

Prior to sending an email to a potential client, you should always have a clear objective and an intended outcome. Think carefully about the type of email you want to send to each potential client before rushing ahead and dashing emails off quickly.

First of all, intended audience is very important. Effective communicators customize every email the best they can, rather than just sending template or generic emails. Tailoring your message to the person you are writing to tells them that you are paying attention to their personal style and concerns. Communicating with customers this way is just another way of making them feel special and comfortable, and ensuring their purchase experience is the best it can be.

Your emails should carry a different tone, depending on the person you're sending them to. For example, the types of emails that you send to colleagues may not be appropriate for your manager or customers. And even emails to customers should be personalized to suit the type of relationship you have with them.

Here are two examples of emails I sent to clients I was in negotiations with at month-end, both of them trying to close the deal to make our monthly target, but each in a slightly different style and each one focusing on the individual customer's situation and needs.

Sean, we need this deal!

I've reworked the numbers with our senior manager on the vehicle in stock. It is a $71,950 vehicle, including all the technology features available.

Instead of the previous quote of $1,527 per month, we will do $1,459. This is not much more than the $1,383 on the less equipped model we quoted on before.

It's black on black, your preferred color, with the full technology and executive packages.

Can we now proceed?

Mr. McDonald, thanks again for your continued loyalty. I do remember your fifth lease from us three years ago.

We would like to make it number six today!

Enclosed is the quote on the 2015 RC350 F Sport model.

This factors in 24,000 km/yr. and uses the incentive available to cover all your up-front costs, including your first month's payment.

Normally the payment would be $793 plus taxes, but for your loyalty we will make it $740.

Please let me know which colors are of interest as supply is limited and the incentives do expire at the end of the month!

Of course, different kinds of emails should be sent to those with whom you've built a rapport, than to those whom you've never met before. Likewise, emails to clients who are senior executives should differ from emails to, say, a local contractor. This is not to suggest an executive is a more important client, but to point out that you should always take into account the customer's communication style, including their language and overall tone.

Personalizing your emails may not always be possible and sometimes mass generic emails are necessary, but the expected outcomes will be vastly different. For example, when I was a partner in an advertising agency, we purchased email lists and targeted thousands of clients with the hope of realizing a one to three percent return, which is typical for that type of marketing.

Contrary to what you might expect, I actually found template-style emails to be more effective when we had already met, contacted or previously conducted business with these potential clients. I've seen this work for various sales organizations where I've worked. I've used template-style emails successfully as a follow-up tool, to announce specific sale events, incentives and time-sensitive promotions.

With my most recent email test, I sent a template email announcement to just thirty potential clients (with whom I'd already engaged) to announce a dealership private sale and I closed eight deals, or twenty-seven percent, within three days. Use template email strategies for very specific purposes: for invitations and to promote time-sensitive events with a clear hook; you don't want to constantly send general mass emails that will turn other potential clients off down the road.

Subject Lines

Keep the subject line short and succinct—no more than ten words if possible. This will be your hook in getting the client's attention, so it should be long enough to convey key information, plus it provides you with some keywords to use as search criteria when sending follow-up emails. However, it's important to keep the subject as tight and concise as possible to provoke interest.

Following are some different kinds of subject lines, each one used for a different purpose, along with some examples of each to illustrate.

The How-to subject line:
- How to take advantage of March incentives.
- How to make your best deal this month!
- How to get the best trade-in value now.
- How to maximize your benefits and make your best deal.

The how-to subject line works well because it appeals to the curiosity of potential customers and implies that they will gain benefits or practical knowledge from opening and reading your email.

The Discover subject line:

- Discover the amazing benefits of doing business with (ABC) company.
- Discover how to make your best deal during this month's sales event.
- Discover the incentives and conveniences available when you become a valued customer.
- Discover additional perks and benefits of becoming an exclusive customer.
- Discover ten reasons that make (ABC's) customer service different.

The discover subject line is aimed at being fascinating and compelling. It is intended to pique the potential customer's curiosity, implying that some inside information is being shared with them, thus motivating them to open and read the email for a better response rate.

The Quick Tips subject line:

- Five quick tips on safe winter driving.
- Quick tips on fuel conservation.
- Quick, healthy gardening tips for the summer.
- Quick tips on healthy dieting.
- Quick tips on getting more for your trade-in vehicle and making your best deal.

At the dealership where I currently work, we publish a quarterly newsletter with quick tips on service, safety and even recipes.

Our open and click-through rates are often over forty percent (more than twice the industry average). One of the contributing reasons is because customers love convenient lists and tips. They don't take a lot of time to read and they offer up useful, practical suggestions. Incorporate "Quick tips" in your subject line with valuable lists and realize a significant open and appreciation rate from your clients.

The Invitation subject line:
- You Are Invited to Our Exclusive Club Lexus Event
- You Are Invited to Preview the All-New Lexus NX
- You Are Invited to Our Grand Opening
- You Are Invited to Our Exclusive Demonstrator Vehicle Promotion
- You're Invited to our Exclusive Private Sale

The invitation subject line can be very effective. It's generally used less often, so when you do use it, it tends to gather higher response rates and bigger turnouts. Clients like and appreciate invitations from familiar places they do business with. Response rates are often higher when these events are well put together, and in your email invitation you include the offer of food, entertainment and prizes.

The four types of subject lines and examples above can be used effectively to target potential clients whom you've engaged with at least once. I still send hundreds of lease-renewal emails and will make reference to the client's account in the subject line because it piques their interest. As a result, I get a consistently high response due to that important lease account reference. Following are some other kinds of subject lines I use almost every day.

- Mr. and Mrs. Jones: Lease Expiring March 25, 2015, on 2012 LEXUS RX350

- 90-Day Notice for Upcoming Lease Renewal on your 2011 ES350
- Follow-up on Test Drive of 2015 GS350 from January 10
- Quick Recap of February 2 Appointment Regarding Finance Options
- Follow-up Regarding Finance/ACT # 123456 (IS250), Mr. Smith

The key to composing the best possible subject line is knowing which category the client falls into in terms of their status as a lead. For example, various clients might be interested in lease renewal options or pre-owned vehicles; with others you may be confirming an appointment or meeting, making a lien payout request, or forwarding a copy of the purchase agreement; obviously each of these different types of leads and customers will require very different subject lines to be clear about what you are communicating to them. Take a few seconds to review the status of your clients so that you can choose an appropriate subject line.

Try inserting the kinds of personalized, informative subject lines we've been talking about in this chapter in the next 100 emails you send and test the response rate from your own mini-experiment. Testing and monitoring results should be a regular part of your marketing strategy. And you should find that writing subject lines with a clear purpose, customized to your intended audience, will make a big difference to the effectiveness of your email communications.

Opening Sentence

Like the subject line, your opening sentence should always be short and succinct with a strong hook to grab the reader's attention right away. They say in journalism, don't bury the lead. The same is true in email communications: Get right to the point so the reader is clear on the purpose of your message. Your clients will appreciate your efficiency and clarity and you'll come across as a true professional.

Here are some strong sample opening sentences:

- The purpose of this email is to notify you that the new model 2015 NX you inquired about is now in inventory and available for you to test drive.
- This email is a follow-up to my earlier voice mail to update you on some newly announced incentives available for the month of March.
- This email is to let you know that your new vehicle has arrived and we would like to schedule delivery to you at your convenience within the next three days.

The follow-up or second sentence should keep the client engaged in the email. Keep it direct and crisp to keep the reader moving along, and eliminate any unnecessary, weak-sounding or negative words.

Here are some examples of effective follow-up sentences:

- My aim is to briefly discuss your needs and requirements in a new vehicle so I may better assist you in choosing your best options.
- Our goal is to assist you in making the best selection for your needs.
- Our focus is on providing you with the best lease, purchase and service options within your budget.
- Please let me know when you have a few minutes available today or tomorrow to discuss your options further.
- Your response today or tomorrow is appreciated. In case I don't hear back from you, I will reconnect within forty-eight hours.

The Main Body of Your Message

In sales, especially when providing quotes or negotiating, the last thing you want to do is use long paragraphs to explain your deal or proposal. You want to keep the details as clear and simple as possible. Use point form or bullet points to make your main points instead of explaining everything at great length; clients will be able to glean quickly the essential details of your proposal. Following is a sample format for the main message of an email:

> As discussed, here is a summary of features and benefits of the 2015 RX350:
>
> - A full complement of luxury, safety and comfort features including navigation, premium leather, lane departure and blind spot monitoring system
> - Comprehensive four-year warranty, including service plan
> - Forty-eight months lease @ $699/month with only $2,000 due at signing
> - Loyalty incentives including waiver of first payment and security deposit
> - Immediate delivery of your first color choice, silver mica

Tone and Grammar

The tone of your email is just as important as the content. Maintain professionalism at all times. Avoid slang, silliness and negativity, even if you've already established a healthy rapport with your client.

Often, quotes and proposals are shared with and reviewed by family or business colleagues, so don't let your guard down or cut corners. Check your wording and grammar, always run a spell check, and double check the spelling of all names in the email before sending. Lastly, include a relevant signature that identifies you and your business as well as your contact information.

The Wrap-up

You should always end your emails with a call to action or next action steps. Set a follow-up time and date where appropriate so that your prospects treat your email with greater seriousness and urgency and with an expectation of a follow-up. Here's an example of an effective wrap-up:

> Please advise when you have a few minutes available in the next day or two to review and I'll follow-up accordingly. Should I not hear from you, I'll plan to reconnect in seventy-two hours.

Effective Emails Get Results

The three testimonials below are the direct result of good email follow up, where my keeping in touch with the clients while giving them space resulted in deals. The clients were very satisfied with the model choices, the purchase experience and my personal communication with them.

> "I found Everold to be prompt and respectful in responding to my questions by email and in person and not 'pushy' ... or trying to speed up my process. This was important to me as I worked through my decision about which car to purchase on my time frame."

> "The sales representative was very helpful and patient with the process. I found that he responded quickly to emails and was able to provide answers to any questions I had. The dealership and the representative made my first car buying experience stress-free and easy."

> "I loved the previous Lexus RX and the salesperson I dealt with assisted me to get another. We are over

three hours away from the dealership we leased from originally and would have been much closer to go to a local dealer. But our sales guy made it very convenient over the phone and by email. I would buy from this dealership again as the experience with Everold was easy and convenient."

EFFECTIVE PHONE AND VOICEMAIL STRATEGIES

Even though it's great to be tech-savvy, don't just text or send emails when you should actually be calling. In recent years, the quality of business communications has deteriorated as people avoid phone calls and face-to-face meetings. As a rule, I will make a call first to try and connect with a client immediately and, if I can't reach them, then I can leave a detailed voicemail (it's often effective to send a follow-up email as well, which we'll cover below).

> Problems and deals are more difficult and time consuming when you are using only text and emails, whereas a phone call helps to resolve and/or clarify issues and close deals more efficiently.

Problems and deals are more difficult and time consuming when you are using only text and emails, whereas a phone call helps to resolve and/or clarify issues and close deals more efficiently. Always try the direct approach first, and follow-up with an email.

Before you pick up the phone to make a call, it's important always to have your plan ready, with the key points outlined to avoid stumbling in case you have to leave a voicemail. If no one picks up, you're better able to address the key points and remain focused doing so.

The Introduction

The most effective voicemails always start with a clear introduction of who's calling, with first and last name, company name, contact number and, if you were referred, a referral name. Referrals in retail sales and specifically automotive retail are always some of the best connections and often lead to some of the easiest deals made, so always ask for referrals and use them, especially when making that connection in a phone call or voicemail.

Here are a couple strong ways to start off your voicemail:

- Hello or good afternoon, Mr. or Mrs. Prospect. This is John Smith with ABC Toyota at (123) 456-7890. I was referred to you by Bob Brown (if there's a referral).

- Good morning, Mr. or Mrs. Jones. Thank you for visiting our showroom earlier to drive and compare our new models.

These short, succinct introductions provide your prospect with good, concise connection details, making the client more attentive to the rest of your message.

Purpose of the Call

When making a call or leaving a voicemail, make the best use of your prospect's time by being as direct as possible when delivering your message. The purpose of this call should be to make that key connection and to learn about the prospect. Avoid wishy-washy words and phrases, such as maybe, wanting, hoping, trying, I was wondering, etc.

Following are some strong, direct ways to convey the purpose of your call:

- The purpose of my call is to get an understanding of the current status of your car, including mileage and service history, so I can review your current lease account status and advise you accordingly.

- Mr. Jones, I'm following up to invite you to our exclusive upgrade sale event on Saturday March 25. As I mentioned in our earlier correspondence, I promised to notify you about our next promotion.

When leaving a voicemail, it's recommended that you make reference to any earlier emails or voicemails if you attempted contact with the prospect before. Reminding them that you've already reached out to them will create more urgency and shows that you are consistent in your approach. However, do not state in your current message that you will follow up with another email or voicemail; that may give the customer an excuse to ignore your current call.

Always keep it brief and don't leave too many details to confuse or to overburden the prospect. Your aim should be for a prospect to call you back to get into the details or to schedule an appointment to meet. If leaving voicemail messages makes you feel nervous, causing you to ramble, then write down the key points to cover before placing the call.

Before closing the voicemail, restate your contact phone number or email and make references to referrals, if any, to increase your credibility.

You can end your voice mail by saying, "Please let me know by email or phone when you have a few minutes and I will follow up accordingly," or say, "Thank you for your time, I look forward to speaking with you." Showing appreciation in your voicemails always leaves a good impression. Your potential clients are more likely to return a call from someone who sounds pleasant and courteous rather than stiff or too businesslike.

VOICEMAIL WITH EMAIL FOLLOW-UP

It's often a good idea to leave a voicemail for your client first and then follow up by email. Contacting your clients by phone first is a nice, personal and immediate way of communicating and, if you can't reach them, you can leave them a message to let them know you called. I like to follow up a voicemail with an email within about fifteen minutes. It's wise to use both options because your client may not be able to take the call right away, (if they are in a meeting or boarding an airplane, for example), but they can usually respond to emails from almost anywhere. I often have clients respond quickly via email just to acknowledge receipt and to establish a future time to connect.

For best results, wait about fifteen minutes after leaving a voicemail before you follow up via email, giving the potential client some time to return the call. And you certainly want to make sure your email complements and aligns with your voice-mail for maximum effect. Mention in your voicemail that you will be following up with a corresponding email; and in your email subject line or the very first line of your message, state that you're following up on the voicemail you left recently.

SUMMARY

- **Always have a clear objective or intended outcome for your emails.** You should have a clear reason for sending every email and should communicate that to the client in your message. Be sure to make the email appropriate to the person it's intended for; match the tone and language of your messages to the various communications styles of your clients.

- **Use template emails for invitations and to promote time-sensitive events.** As long as they have a clear hook, these types of generic emails can work well in these situations; however, avoid constantly sending mass emails to cover all customers and situations; that will turn off potential clients down the road.

- **Keep the subject line short and to the point,** usually up to ten words; this is your hook to get the client's attention. You can also use informative subject lines as search criteria when hunting for specific emails or following up.

- **The how-to subject line** works well; it makes potential customers feel like they are gaining practical information.

- **The discover subject line** is aimed at being fascinating and compelling to pique the potential customer's curiosity, which can lead to a better open and response rate.

- **Incorporate "quick tips" in your subject line** to increase your open rates and levels of engagement. Clients love valuable lists and tips that don't take much time to read.

- **The invitation subject line** is appreciated by clients, when coming from familiar places they do, or intend to do, business with. Response rates can be even higher when your invitation includes an offer of food, refreshments, special offers and prizes.

- **The key to the subject line** is knowing what category of lead your prospective client falls into. Take a few seconds to review the status of your clients before emailing them to choose the most appropriate subject line.

- **Your opening sentence** should always be short and to the point with a strong hook to grab the client's attention.

- **The follow-up or second sentence** should keep the client engaged in the email; eliminate any unnecessary, weak or negative wording.

- **Format and organize your main message** using point form or bullet points to discuss key points instead of explaining them at great length. Your client will be able to scan and quickly get the substance of your proposal.

- **The tone and grammar** of your email are just as important as the content, so ensure that you maintain professionalism and avoid slang even if you've already established rapport.

- **Always end your emails with an expectation or next action step.** Set a follow-up time and date so your prospect treats your email with a little more urgency and an expectation of a follow-up.

- **Direct phone calls are often more effective than emails** especially when you want to get a better sense of the client's emotional reaction. You can gauge buyers' emotions much better by direct contact, either in person or via phone calls, than you can through texts and emails.

- Before you pick up the phone to make a call, it's important **always to have your plan ready** with your key points outlined, especially if you have to leave a message.

- The most **effective voicemails always start with a clear introduction** of who's calling, including first and last name, company name, contact number and, if you were referred, a referral name.

- When making a call or leaving a voice mail, **make the best use of your prospect's time** and be as direct as possible.

- **Always keep your voicemails brief** and don't leave too many details to confuse or to overburden the prospect. Remember, what you really want is for them to call you back to get into the details or to schedule an appointment.

- **Wrap up properly:** Before closing the voicemail, you should also restate your contact phone number or email and make references to referrals, if any, to increase your credibility.

- **Send an email within fifteen minutes** of leaving a voicemail to cover all your bases and increase the chances of the client getting back to you. Make sure your email complements and aligns with your voicemail for maximum effect.

CHAPTER 10

MAXIMIZE OPPORTUNITIES AND GO THE EXTRA MILE

Throughout this book, we've looked at the fundamental principles you must follow to achieve ultimate success in sales. By now you should be well aware of the key processes and techniques you need to master to become a high-performing sales professional: things such as making that all-important positive first impression and connection, a commitment to making daily progress, a desire to add more value than anyone else, creating an action plan, turning objections into opportunities and practicing small daily rituals that create a state of mind for success, among many others.

Now that we've explored the answers to the how and the why of sales excellence, I hope you have a better understanding of what separates top performing sales reps and organizations from the rest.

Beyond the specific strategies and tactics we've looked at to this point, there are a few other qualities that make the difference between being good at your job and delivering excellence in everything that you do. These are the intangibles of excellence as a sales professional.

As the forty-second president of the United States, Bill Clinton once said, in a speech on policy making at Georgetown University in April 2014, "The details matter and they will have consequences." The daily details and rituals in sales definitely matter, and eventually lead to bigger and better success.

PERSEVERANCE

Through twenty-five years in retail sales and marketing, and from all the research and training I've conducted, I'm convinced that more than half of what separates the successful from the mediocre is perseverance. Most people will say they go the extra mile but do they really? According to Steve Jobs, former CEO of Apple, "The extra mile is usually a lonely place with very few people there, but it's the place filled with the opportunities."

I've experienced this loneliness to a point while writing this book late at night, early mornings before going into work, and on weekends. In order to achieve ultimate success, you must approach things differently. I didn't have to undertake such a big project as a requirement of my job, but writing this book has enabled me to master and appreciate the art and science of sales more deeply and proficiently that simply doing the job ever could. Although I have enough knowledge and experience to manage dealerships and train sales professionals, writing a book on the topic has taken me the extra mile in my own journey of professional development.

Going the extra mile is all about taking initiative on your own, and having the perseverance to continue improving what you do and how you do it, no matter how lonely or difficult that may seem at times. There were many other projects I started and almost finished, giving up somewhere along the way. Writing this book won't be one of them.

To have success, sometimes you have to be prepared to start early, work late, make those extra phone calls and send those extra emails. You have to try to help a teammate who needs some encouragement or a client who needs some extra help or advice. You have to be willing to give all you've got when the month-end or year-end target is on the line. Instead of throwing in the towel when faced with an ambitious target for your dealership, how about persevering through it and pushing to achieve it, for everyone's benefit?

Sending extra emails and making more calls have always netted me more new deals and I've never waited to be asked to do these things. I've always set my own targets and standards, even closing my door sometimes, just to get more done.

> I'm convinced that more than half of what separates the successful from the mediocre is perseverance.

To separate yourself is often harder than fitting in, but that's what makes you different and leads to bigger success.

USE YOUR TIME WISELY

The most precious resource we have is time. So why do salespeople waste so much of it, standing around and waiting for the next client to show up or for the phone to ring?

We often operate on deadlines, such as mid-month and month-end results, but why wait to get things going? Why not get things started and accomplished sooner instead of using deadlines as a way to manage your activities?

Now, I'm as guilty of procrastinating as the next person sometimes. At Lexus, we have monthly sales quizzes available online at the first of each month, and I always leave them to the last minute, sometimes the last day of the month, to complete.

This is an example of allowing time to impose its will on me when it should be the other way around; to be more effective and productive, we have to take control of our time, becoming more efficient and freeing up more time to get other, perhaps bigger, things accomplished.

CHOOSE THE PEOPLE AROUND YOU WISELY

If you're working in a retail sales environment like an auto dealership, with bosses, staff and even clients who make you unhappy and hold you back, maybe it's time to adjust or move on. If people around you create a negative work environment, you need to make a change. Surround yourself with kind, hardworking people instead of those who are miserable, constant complainers and unproductive. Take better control of your situation and associate yourself with visionaries to help you to succeed.

Teams in business win because their most talented innovators and visionaries are willing to help others be better. They always know their role (as explained earlier in chapter 3, Best Practices of Top Sales Performers) and sometimes they set aside personal goals in the greater interest of the team. Many months during the year, when a couple of us on the sales floor would have exceeded our monthly targets and could have carried over deals to the following month, we found ways to deliver those vehicles before the month-end, sometimes at a disadvantage to us individually, but providing a benefit to the sales team as a whole by enabling the dealership to hit the overall monthly targets.

RESET: LEARN FROM YOUR FAILURES

Whenever we've had underperforming months or failed to hit targets, the reasons are always very predictable. Common excuses include: the weather was bad, the market was tough, finance and lease rates were too high or other manufacturers had better incentives or new models. Occasionally circumstances completely beyond our control will cause us to fail, but most often it's our own approach that leads us to failure.

Failures are sometimes unavoidable, and they're okay as long as you learn from them. I've personally had two business failures and take responsibility regardless of whether I was in complete control or not. The fact is, if I knew then what I know now, things would have been different. Be prepared to re-innovate and remarket based on what you learn from your mistakes. Most successful people in life have failed numerous times. Rather than letting failure define them, they embrace it, take responsibility for it and learn from it.

Occasionally circumstances completely beyond our control will cause us to fail, but most often it's our own approach that leads us to failure.

One month recently, I personally had lower than expected sales results and the only person I blamed was myself. However, the next month started off with a bang because I won't allow myself to make the same mistakes two months in a row. I will re-innovate and revisit my marketing strategies to ensure success going forward.

INITIATIVE AND INNOVATION

In chapter 5, we focused on innovation and marketing as important, key practices for ultimate sales and business success. Fear of failure, rejection and the unknown always stop people from sharing or executing their ideas.

If you fail to take action then they aren't ideas to begin with. Make sure you step up, participate or execute your ideas to increase your chances of sales and business success. The simple fact is that some of those ideas, if tried, would have worked. So trust your instincts, have faith in your abilities and don't wait for things to happen: innovate, innovate and innovate.

CHASE EXPERIENCES, NOT MATERIAL POSSESSIONS

I'll confess that, like many people, I've been caught up in the quest for material possessions at one time or another, and for a while that may seem rewarding. But I've learned that chasing material possessions is less important than chasing the experiences that lead to ultimate success, which also taught me to commit myself to Kaizen to improve myself personally and professionally even a little bit every day.

Writing this book is a good example. In the introduction, I admitted to being impatient when reading books, let alone writing one. Now that I'm near the end, I can tell you that I've enjoyed the writing experience, the research, the discussions and the many encouragements from colleagues like Matt Marelli and Michael Panchyson that have led me to this point. This book has been fifteen years in the making and I thought about it for an entire year before I even began the fourteen-month writing process; I've dedicated a lot of time and energy to this project, but now I can say it has been well worth it.

Sure, it's rewarding to hold my finished book in my hands and to be able to share this tangible work with the world, but much of the value for me is less in the end product and more in the actual process of creating it. The journey from idea to book has allowed me to connect and collaborate with other professionals, to think deeply about my own experience, and to understand my field in new ways.

Similarly, being successful in your sales role may allow you to drive a more luxurious car and acquire all kinds of material possessions, and there's nothing wrong with that. But I recommend that you also savor the journey, take pride in your work, fulfillment from your accomplishments along the way and satisfaction from knowing that you will never stop improving and developing professionally.

GIVING BACK

Accomplishing ultimate success in whatever we do professionally is always great and can provide wealth and a great deal of flexibility and personal satisfaction. But the best type of success I've experienced is a by-product of personal and professional success—and that's giving back to others. Giving back or getting involved in your community—or helping those who are less fortunate—can provide you with tremendous happiness and fulfillment. Whatever you accomplish professionally or personally, always keep in mind the impact you can make to the less fortunate, even if it's on a small scale or simply by volunteering your time. Whenever you're at your best, you're giving, so step up and give and enjoy real success.

THE GIFT OF KNOWLEDGE

As I mentioned before, I have found writing this book immensely challenging and fulfilling. My satisfaction is in the completion of a process, something I started from scratch that took me on a rewarding, if sometimes difficult, journey. My hope is that the knowledge I've gained over a long sales career, and shared with you here in *The Reid Method*, will help you on your own professional journey—to constantly improve your expertise, your practices and yourself. I hope that the fundamentals and best practices of effective sales techniques that you've read about in these pages will improve your chances of sales success.

If I sell thousands of copies of this book, that would be gratifying; but even if I don't, the more important thing will be that
I've helped other sales professionals to position themselves for
success—and the most important thing will be to say, I did it!

SUMMARY

- **The small daily details and rituals in sales matter,** and
  eventually lead to bigger and better success.

- **What separates the successful from the mediocre is
  perseverance:** Most people will say they go the extra mile,
  but few send that last email, make that extra phone call,
  come in a bit early or stay a little later to get the results,
  and that's why the extra mile sometimes is a lonely place.

- **Use your time wisely:** The most precious resource we have
  is time. Don't allow time to pass idly by and impose its will
  on you; manage your time better to accomplish more every
  day.

- **Choose the people around you wisely:** Take better control
  of your situation and associate yourself with visionaries to
  help you to succeed.

- **Learn from your failures:** Occasionally circumstances completely beyond our control will cause us to fail, but most
  often it's our own approach that leads us to failure. Learn
  from your failures as a building block for success.

- **Initiative and innovation:** The initial failure is in not trying
  to execute your ideas. If you fail to take action then they ar-
  en't ideas to begin with. Make sure you step up, participate
  or execute your ideas to increase your chances of sales
  and business success.

- **Chase experiences, not material possessions:** Savor the journey, take pride in your work and fulfillment from your accomplishments along the way.

- **Kaizen your career:** Dedicate yourself to continuously improving and developing professionally, and take satisfaction from the process.

- **Giving Back:** the best type of success I've experienced is a by-product of personal and professional success—and that's giving back to others. As Tony Robbins said in one of his coaching seminars, the secret to living is in giving.

The Reid Method is my gift to you. I hope you will use it for years to come and refer to it often—to help you on your journey of continuous professional development, and to sales success!

ABOUT THE AUTHOR

Everold Reid is a veteran sales professional who continues to redefine what it takes to achieve sales mastery in the competitive world of automotive, advertising and marketing sales. As a passionate and award-winning salesperson, he has remained at the top of his game for more than two-and-a-half decades by applying proven sales methods and strategies, many of which were self taught.

In 1989, Everold took a summer job selling cars to earn extra money to put himself through college. He recognized early on that he possessed a gift for selling, and his summer job soon evolved into a full-time career in automotive sales. He hasn't looked back.

From his earliest days in sales to the present, Everold has constantly challenged himself to expand his knowledge about his chosen profession. He regularly studies the world's top sales professionals to continuously learn from the best. Everold applies the Kaizen philosophy of continuous improvement to all of his sales, advertising and marketing activities.

In addition to sales strategies and techniques, Everold possesses extensive marketing expertise in the retail automotive and advertising industry. For several years, Everold partnered in and managed a marketing company with clients across North America and the Caribbean. He has initiated unique and strategic marketing partnerships with major companies such as Aeroplan and worked with celebrities and local non-profit groups, including the Michael "Pinball" Clemons Foundation and Kerr Street Mission in Oakville, Ontario. He has devised print, radio and TV campaigns and utilized the latest digital tools to give the dealerships he represents an edge. His advice and insights on automotive selling, advertising and marketing are sought after by some of the world's top automotive brands, including Toyota and Lexus.

More recently, Everold has broadened his career path to include business coaching, mentoring and speaking engagements. Whether it's a sales team that needs to reset its strategic goals and objectives or a corporation in search of high-powered motivational messages to share with its sales teams, Everold is available as a business coach or a mentor. He is also available for speaking engagements at your place of business, whether it's a Fortune 500 company, an automotive dealership (or group), a government agency or an educational institution.

CONTACT US

Everold Reid is available as a business coach, consultant or mentor, as well as for seminars and speaking engagements, to help boost you and your sales team to higher levels of performance.

Whether your sales team needs to reset its strategic goals and objectives, or your organization is in search of high-powered motivational messages to share with your sales teams, Everold and The Reid Method can help you achieve sales mastery.

No matter what kind of organization you are—a Fortune 500 company, an automotive dealership (or group), a government agency or an educational institution—The Reid Method can work for you. Contact us today to learn more about how you can take your sales success to new heights.

Email: everold@thereidmethod.com
Website: www.thereidmethod.com
Facebook: https://www.facebook.com/thereidmethod
Twitter: https://twitter.com/TheReidMethod
LinkedIn: https://ca.linkedin.com/in/everoldreid